"Tim's book nails the eight characteristics of high-performing teams. These characteristics are about relationships and culture, rather than just the task at hand. I call it ignoring the scoreboard and focusing on the process—all the things that go into doing your job, minimizing errors, trusting your teammates to do the same—and at the end of the 80 minutes or financial year—then look up and see what the scoreboard tells you! My experience in life is by getting the process right, the scoreboard looks after itself."

Nick Farr-Jones AM, *former Wallaby Captain and Great*

"The secret of the All Blacks' success is that there is no secret—it comes down to hard work and application. The current players follow a proud legacy of success and it's a legacy they strive to replicate and enhance. As our national sport, New Zealand's identity as a nation is very much tied up with our success on the field.

Good coaching, talent, work ethic, and correct fit are critically important, of course, but the right mindset and application are key to success in any team, or any endeavor in life.

Tim Baker explains this perfectly in this very readable and practical book that is easily applied to your team."

Grant Fox MBE, *former All Black Legend and CEO, Techfront NZ*

"Tim Baker does a wonderful job dismantling the mystique of continued and sustainable success. He creates guidelines that some leaders think they already possess. ... Mistakenly."

Tom Lawton, *former Wallaby Great*

"An organisation is only as good as its people and their accomplishments, and challenges can help shape the future direction and successes of an organisation. For these people to do great work, they need to feel part of a team and a great team at that. The value of teamwork cannot be underestimated – it is vital to your organisation's success.

Tim Baker writes a practical book that is guaranteed to lead to higher performance."

Commissioner Katarina Carroll, *Queensland Police Service*

WINNING TEAMS

The Eight Characteristics of High Performing Teams

TIM BAKER

To the game they play in heaven and all those who've

played, are playing, or are about to play.

CONTENTS

INTRODUCTION

Most team problems can be traced back to a simple misunderstanding, communication breakdown, or relationship malfunction. It's the people dimension—not the task dimension—that continually challenges team leaders. *Winning Teams: The Eight Characteristics of a High-Performing Team* offers leaders practical and easy-to-implement tools to profile and build a robust team identity. A brand-new team identity model sets this book apart from other books on team development.

The *Team Identity Model* consists of the eight research-based characteristics that separate high-performing from low-performing teams. The focus of the model is the often-neglected people dimension of teamwork. The secret of a winning team is found in how its members relate and interact with one another and the frequency of their collaboration.

All high-performing teams have a strong team identity. A winning team identity doesn't happen by chance; identity is something that's purposely built by great teams. Team identity is what makes a great team great. It's not a marketing slogan or fad. Robust team identity is based on an unbreakable bond and laser-like purpose that are shared by the members. How team members relate to

one another and how the team interacts with its stakeholders personify its identity. Teamwork is two-dimensional: task and people. Team identity is largely shaped
by the people dimension.

These eight characteristics or attributes focus on the
people dimension to enable superior performance. The
model offers a fresh blueprint for leaders looking to boost
team performance.

Illustrations of team identity and its characteristics in
action are drawn from the world's most successful sporting team—the New Zealand All Blacks. The All Blacks
are the most successful rugby team in history. Many good
judges believe this team to be the most successful sports
team, in any code, ever. In 112 years of playing rugby, New
Zealand's winning percentage is 78. What's the All Blacks'
secret formula? It turns out that it's not so secret. What
can the lesser-known teams in the world of work learn
and apply from the success of this great sporting team?

The lessons are transferrable from the playing field
to the worksite. A raft of research is emerging telling us
that it's not the task dimension that sets great teams apart
from the mediocre—it's the relationship dimension. The
differentiator between low- and high-performing teams
is the quality and regularity of the interactions between
members. Teams fail because they don't invest enough
time and energy in teamwork, not taskwork.

Team development, however, is more than an outdoor ropes course—aside from the laughter, merriment,
and temporary morale boost it can manufacture. Building a positive and hearty team identity is daily, deliberate
work. It's fun, too. But this type of fun is less superficial
and more sustainable—it's the elation that heightened
and continual team performance brings.

We know that there are certain characteristics all high-performing teams have in common. Team identity is built from three functions: *buffering, bridging*, and *building*. The eight characteristics support these three functions. Working together, these three functions and the eight characteristics form a framework for accelerating team performance, emphasizing the people dimension of teamwork. By applying the model, your team will redress the typical imbalance of too much task focus and too little people focus.

Building trust, sharing leadership, being agile, creating purpose, managing stakeholders, improving systems, utilizing diversity, and *learning continuously* are the eight characteristics of a superior team. The model offers leaders the most comprehensive design of team identity found in the team literature.

A team's identity fosters trust or distrust, promotes or suppresses agility, and boosts or blows performance. Several practical and easy-to-implement tools to build a healthy team identity, emphasizing the often-neglected people dimension of teamwork, populate *Winning Teams*.

The book is broken into three parts. *PART I—Building a robust team identity* is based on the simple but often overlooked premise that a team is a bunch of people working toward a shared goal. With a dose of common sense, and backed by reputable research, we explore the idea that it's the people dimension of the team that shapes a strong team identity and makes the difference in team success. Team identity is the secret sauce for high performance.

PART II considers the eight characteristics of high performance in depth and how to optimize each attribute. Practical tools to assist a leader to get the very best from their team are spelled out in detail in the second part of *Winning Teams*.

And *PART III* explains how to construct a profile of your team. You can access a 360-degree diagnostic to assess your team against these characteristics. The strengths and opportunities for growth identified from the team evaluation report provide a useful platform for developing a manageable, action-based pathway to higher performance. PART III brings it all together and creates the roadmap for building a powerful team identity for your team.

Winning Teams is for team leaders—usually promoted into leadership for their technical know-how—who often struggle with the people dimension of their managerial role. To add to the demands of leadership, business rewards task achievement, whether it's more sales, producing better widgets, or superior service delivery. The emphasis is on technical capability and task accomplishment, when it's the people factor that transforms a team from mediocre to magnificent.

Concentrating on the people dimension transforms team performance. But as all team leaders recognize, it's the interpersonal interaction and engagement aspect that's most challenging. It's the people dimension, ironically, that has the greatest impact on task success or failure.

Unsurprisingly, leaders are looking for clear, coherent models and practical and easy-to-implement tools to improve human collaboration, based on sound social science. *Winning Teams* fills the void.

PART I

Building a robust team identity

CHAPTER 1

What can business learn from the world's greatest sporting team?

When the opposition line up against the New Zealand national rugby team—the All Blacks—they face the "haka," the highly ritualized challenge thrown down by one group of warriors to another. Māori believe that the haka draws up "tīpuna," their ancestors, from the earth to the soul. It summons them to aid them in their struggles here on earth, with the sound of "ngunguru," the low rumble of an earthquake:

> 'Tis death! 'tis death!
> I may die! I may die!
> 'Tis life! 'tis life!
> I might live! I might live!

Opposing teams face the haka in different ways. Some try to ignore it, others advance on it, most stand shoulder to shoulder to face it. Whatever their outward response, inwardly the opposition know that they are standing before more than a collection of 15 individual players. They are facing a culture, an identity, an ethos, a belief system—and a collective passion and purpose beyond anything they have faced before.

Often, by the time the haka reaches its crescendo, the opposition have already lost. For rugby, like business and like much of life, is played primarily in the mind.[1]

The All Blacks are the most successful rugby team in history. Many good judges believe this team to be the most successful sports team, in any code, ever. In 112 years of playing rugby, New Zealand's winning percentage is 78. In the 20 years since the sport turned professional, that figure has risen to 84. Those figures are astounding and speak for themselves. The All Blacks are clearly doing something right and have been doing so for over a century.

You don't have to be a rugby tragic to appreciate that record!

And if, like me, your country has been on the receiving end of the awesome All Blacks, you probably have a grudging and painful respect for this team. It's an even more impressive record when you consider that the entire population of New Zealand is a touch over four million people.

To appreciate the success of the All Blacks, it helps to understand how it began. In the 1905 tour to Europe and the USA, the All Blacks—or the "Originals," as that side is now known—played 35 matches and won 34, scored 976 points and conceded 59. Impressive start.

Jock Phillips is one of New Zealand's most respected historians. "Rugby really took off as a national game at the turn of the century," Phillips says, "and the crucial thing there was the 1905 All Black team." According to Phillips, New Zealand had—and perhaps still has—a certain insecurity about its place in the world. "We've always got a certain anxiety that we are falling off the edge, that we don't really count." The tour, he says, "gave New Zealanders a sense that they had a role to play in the empire."[2] In so many cases—whether individual or team—success is driven by feelings of diffidence.

What can we learn about teamwork from the All Blacks? How can those lessons be translated to the world of work?

The All Blacks mirror the characteristics of high-performing teams I have studied in the workplace. Whether one understands rugby union or sport in general, one can learn a lot from examining this team. It's clear to all who study the All Blacks that they have made a deliberate effort to build an exemplary team culture.

In this chapter, we look at some of these traits—on and off the field. These themes correlate with the eight characteristics of high-performing teams I cover extensively later in the book.

Teamwork in any context is broadly made up of two dimensions: task and people. The task of any sporting team is to win the competition they're competing in. The All Blacks do this better than any other team in the world. But it's the work they do off the field and in their practices that makes the difference. And a lot of this off-field work is about building the people dimension.

Although unquestionably skillful, the All Black's point of difference is the culture they create within the team. This work is mostly done off the field.

What the All Blacks do on the field is inspirational (if you are a supporter and not on the losing team!) and highly effective. But it's what they do off the field that contributes significantly to what they do on the field. And I'm not just referring to training and practice sessions.

But something was wrong in 2004. The 2003 World Cup had gone badly for the All Blacks. By the beginning of the following year, senior players were threatening to leave the team. Discipline was poor. A drinking culture prevailed. Systems and processes were disorderly. A poor culture existed and needed a radical transformation.

In response, a fresh management team under Graham Henry, the new head coach, began rebuilding the world's most successful sporting team from the inside out. Henry wanted a different culture, a culture that placed emphasis on individual character and personal leadership.

Their mantra became *Better People Make Better All Blacks*.

The fruits of this success were sweet: two Rugby World Cup victories four years apart and an incredible win rate of just over 86 percent.

Henry—who confesses to being a natural autocrat—felt there was a need to transfer leadership from coach to players. His argument was simple. The team is the one that plays the game; the players need to lead on and off the field. This meant Henry needed to change his natural leadership style. The traditional *them and us* between coaching staff and players had to become *we*.

And so, transformation began. Leadership groups within the team were formed, giving senior players a distinct portfolio of responsibility. These responsibilities ranged from on-field leadership to social organization to mentoring new players to community relations. Henry contended that leadership and development were best left in the hands of senior players. After all, younger players are more receptive to messages and examples from senior players than from the coach.

The structure of the working week is a good illustration of sharing the leadership. The Sunday evening review meetings of the previous game are facilitated by the coaches, although significant input is now expected from the senior leadership group. Then, over the course of the week leading up to the next game, responsibility and leadership are handed over to the players.

By Thursday, the team's priorities and intensity levels are owned by the players. By the time the All Blacks take the field on Saturday, the players are running the show. Shared leadership is now the norm.

Where the rubber meets the road

**We are the most dominant team
in the history of the world.**

In 2013, an English journalist wandered into New Zealand's team room and saw the statement "We are the most dominant team in the history of the world" written on a whiteboard. It's not far wrong. In the four years since the last World Cup, the All Blacks' winning percentage has risen to 93. Count the defeats on one hand and you will have two digits spare. In the same period, there have twice been two new moons in the space of a single month. The All Blacks really do lose once in a blue moon.[3]

Trust is an essential part of a high-performing team. It sounds easy. But trust is hard to gain and easy to lose, as we know. In the new culture, the All Blacks are openly encouraged to be constructively critical of their fellow teammates. The players review the video replay of the previous game. Everything is out in the open: missed tackles, wayward passes, poorly placed kicks, set plays, and so on. The players can critique what they see on the screen. This is an expectation. Nothing personal, but mistakes are there to see on the big screen. Constructive criticism comes from the players, not the coaches.

Shared leadership characterizes this new culture. It's no longer the coach who is the only one making suggestions and highlighting key points. James Kerr, in his inspirational book *Legacy: What the All Blacks Can Teach Us About the Business of Life*, illustrates this commitment to shared leadership perfectly in a poignant example of mentoring young players coming into the team:

During the World Cup, two new players, Cory Jane and Israel Dagg, decided to have a big night out in a Takapuna Bar. The next day, the New Zealand media called for these two players to be booted from the team. It was painful, humiliating, and embarrassing. The pair had to face the seven most senior players in the team. Out of the media spotlight, they were asked to explain their actions to their heroes growing up, in a private meeting.

> For young men, at the prime of their lives, in the tournament of their dreams, this must have been both mortifying and humbling,[4]

says Kerr. After this confronting and chastening experience, both players decided to make a public apology to the rest of the team and the case was closed. Shared leadership at its best.

Graham Henry—changing direction to revive the team's successes—wanted the team to play with renewed purpose. A set of values was adopted, and a consistent application of storytelling and metaphors, devolved leadership, the creation of a learning environment, and a focus on mental application culminated in his team winning a World Cup. They were back, officially the best rugby team in the world.

Creating a clear purpose gave the players a greater stake in shaping their own team environment. Heightened levels of trust came from more collaborative decision-making. Their motto was *Together we advance.* The All Blacks were vision-driven and value-based.

With more success come greater expectations from devoted fans. Managing these expectations from their fervent public and the communities within New Zealand requires some consideration. The All Blacks' leadership group decides what events they attend and who will represent the team on these occasions. The workload is shared. Through the example of senior players, such as the legendary Richie McCaw, the players recognize their off-field responsibilities and commitments. Each player—idolizing their childhood heroes—comes into the All Black sanctum acutely aware of their new role model status. Managing stakeholders is taken seriously— it's part of the job of an All Black.

There are many rituals and processes that are part and parcel of being an All Black. As Kerr points out,

> Rituals reflect, remind, reinforce, and reignite the central story. They make it real in a vital, visceral way.[5]

Induction ceremonies to first caps, performing the haka before matches, seating positions on the team bus (senior players at the back), post-match debriefings, and feedback sessions are some of these rituals. These systems are the framework that holds the belief system in place. But as I mentioned earlier, they're open to scrutiny and change. Good teams are always fine-tuning their systems and processes.

Rituals aren't confined to sports teams. Sport, like business, is warfare by other means. All high-performing teams need superior systems to win. Just as a tribe of primitive warriors had rituals to galvanize themselves for the heat of battle against the enemy, modern-day teams have procedures and protocol too. The All Blacks' culture of ceremony, symbolism, and narration is not dissimilar to that of combat groups like the US Marine Corps. This ritualization is relevant to high-performing teams in the corporate world, too. What's more, these systems need to evolve to be effective and relevant to the times and circumstances.

The evolution of the Māori haka is a case in point. The haka was almost abolished from the All Blacks' pre-match ritual. The pressure of TV cameras being shoved in players' faces and the fact that the players just wanted to get on and play brought into question the value of this pre-match ritual. Further, the perception that the haka was for Māori people was also a deterrent.

But society is now less tribal. The composition of the All Black teams mirrors a more cosmopolitan society. The team is no longer made up of Europeans and Māori. Tongans, Samoans, Fijians, Europeans, and Māori are all part of the team. This high-performing sporting team—like New Zealand society—has a more diverse ethnic mix. Teams in the corporate world—with the impact of globalization—are also more multi-racial.

A new haka was composed to encompass the more diverse cultural mix of the team. This famous ritual was adapted for the times. Gilbert Enoka, the All Black team sports psychologist, explains this change:

We had to manage the transition between Māori and Pacifica. It wasn't until we sat down and said, tell us what it means to be a New Zealander and tell us what it means to be an All Black ... then all of a sudden it came from a place inside them and had a connection and meaning and ... the whole notion of our parents, your tīpuna buried in the soil and you have a connection to the land and you put the jersey on and you've got a fern on and you're all connected. So, suddenly, your Fijians and Tongans and the Samoans ... could connect with the fact that, yes, this is our time, and this is our moment, and this is my time, and this is my moment.[6]

Like all great teams, the All Blacks improved their processes to suit the times.

As a former teacher, Graham Henry understood the value of learning and the need for continuous development. Sean Fitzpatrick, another legendary All Black and long-serving captain, is a student of success. He believes passionately in lifelong learning and the idea of developing oneself. Fitzpatrick says,

Success is modest improvement, consistently done.[7]

Continuous improvement challenges the status quo, always questioning the way things are done. This applies to both the individual and the team. One of the pillars of the All Black team environment is devotion to learning and development. It's a team constantly on the lookout for the edge, and Sean Fitzpatrick makes the point that this All Black mindset can be applied to business or, indeed, anything in life.

Outstanding leaders in business are always searching for the edge over their competitors, like the All Blacks. And this starts with a culture of continuous learning in all facets of the business.

Throughout *Winning Teams*, some of the characteristics that make the All Blacks the #1 sporting team in the world will be translated into practical solutions to achieving better teamwork. So, to answer the question I posed at the beginning of the chapter: There is a lot we can learn from the All Blacks for organizational success.

In the next chapter, we consider the people dimension as an often-underestimated aspect of teams and its connection to high performance.

CHAPTER 2

Developing unbreakable team relationships: the key to high performance

... for most teams, 80 percent of the leader's attention is on doing the tasks and only 20 percent on developing personal relationships.

Like circus acrobats, team leaders juggle lots of balls in the air at once. Occasionally one of the balls slips through the grasp of the acrobat. Leaders drop the ball too. The show must go on, however. Most leaders pick up the ball and carry on. But unlike the circus acrobat, the leader sometimes isn't aware that the ball's been dropped until later.

For example, two team members are having a minor disagreement. The leader doesn't bother intervening. It seems a mild enough quarrel. It's only later when a shouting match erupts—heard throughout the building—that the leader realizes something is wrong and requires their intervention.

Or, the construction team stops communicating with the contract engineer, a key stakeholder but a pain in the neck. As a result of not talking, the team doesn't receive a *timely and significant change to the construction plan. It's only when the team leader chats casually with the engineer that they realize this change of plan has occurred. The project is derailed.*

Leadership can be a tough juggling act.

Team leaders have two broad responsibilities: making sure the functional tasks are completed and relationships sustained. Dealing with these two responsibilities—task and people—is key to team performance. These dimensions of teamwork involve doing the team tasks efficiently and effectively and fostering an environment in which productive working relationships can flourish.

Although both dimensions are vital for team success, for most teams, 80 percent of the leader's attention is on doing the tasks and only 20 percent on developing personal relationships. Typically, the assumption held is that the people part of teamwork will sort itself out with minimum involvement from the team leader, so the primary focus is on task challenges. False assumption.

Dysfunctional teams are everywhere; they're common. The dysfunction nearly always originates with relationship breakdowns that end in task malfunctions. Would you agree?

What's more, the quality of team relationships impacts on the quality of team performance—just as the All Blacks discovered. Apart from superior technical skills, high-performing teams are characterized by healthy robust working relationships. Team success is a combination of both the task and people dimensions. But it is the attention to the people dimension that is often overlooked.

Two dimensions of team leadership

A useful way of viewing teams is through the lens of task and people. The task dimension involves reaching project milestones or the activities and functions the team is responsible for. The way team members relate and interact with each other is the people dimension. Even though the two dimensions overlap in teamwork, it is useful to understand both.

To make this clear, the task dimension covers matters such as:

- establishing a clear understanding of the work task

- defining milestones and objectives for the task or project

- distributing workloads and responsibilities within the team

- clarifying priorities

- working within the parameters of budgets

- developing reporting procedures and

- doing the work.

The people dimension includes:

- recognizing and adhering to team values

- creating a collaborative and inclusive culture

- understanding and appreciating personalities and preferences

- managing interpersonal conflict

- coaching and supporting others and

- opening channels of communication.

These are not comprehensive lists of activities for either dimension, but they serve to draw a distinction between the two dimensions.

These two dimensions work together. Task and people occur in chorus when a team collaborates on a project or a joint work task. The task and people dimensions are two parts of one whole. Most organizational work involves collaboration between people. Relationships are strengthened or weakened through the experience of taskwork. And it works in reverse too: the quality of task performance largely depends on the condition of the working relationships. Tasks and people are interdependent.

Properly attending to both dimensions improves team performance.

Tasks don't get done automatically—unless they are fully automated—nor do healthy working relationships form by accident. Although more and more tasks are being automated, relationships can't be automated. Both dimensions require consideration, particularly the people aspect. We are told that leaders are responsible for getting the work done with and through other people.

Yet the focus is on the tasks more than on the people. Until an interpersonal crisis erupts, most of the leader's energy is devoted to accomplishing the task. In the early stages of team formation, leaders proactively pay attention to building relationships—often referred to as team building. This stage of team development is what Bruce Tuckman calls the forming stage.[8] Once the team-building program is concluded, it's down to business—the "real" business of getting tasks done. And the people dimension takes a back seat, like a child on a long road trip. But as we know, neglecting the child for too long can disrupt the journey!

Ignoring team relationships disrupts a team's journey, too.

Although both dimensions are important and inseparable, in *Winning Teams*, the accent is mostly on team relationships. Since the people dimension is typically by-passed—after the initial team building ritual—it's given more attention in the pages ahead. This consideration is more than redressing the imbalance between the two dimensions. Increasingly, research is telling us that it's the people dimension that separates low-performing from high-performing teams. We'll look at this in the next chapter.

The people dimension is commonly referred to as *maintenance*. In one sense, it is an apt descriptor. In life, we tend to deal with maintenance issues only when they become problematic, not beforehand. Maintenance is overlooked until it can't be overlooked anymore.

Do you get regular physical check-ups, or do you wait until you experience real discomfort before consulting your GP? Do you ignore the friendly (although sometimes annoying) reminders for your annual dental check-up until you have a sore tooth? Do you regularly maintain your car, changing its oil and checking the tires and water level, or wait for an unfamiliar noise emanating from under the hood? Maintaining relationships—whether personal or work-related—is also often attended to only when frustration or a serious misunderstanding arises.

Relationship maintenance should be ongoing and not occur only when it's apparent there is a breakdown. Regrettably, it often does. I'd love $100 (on top of my consulting fees!) every time I'm invited to do a team-building exercise precipitated by a serious collapse in trust and fractured relationships.

I prefer the term *people* rather than *maintenance* when referring to the non-task dimension of teamwork. Maintenance infers a mechanical process. *People* is more easily understood in a team context. Nonetheless, people and relationships need regular maintenance, particularly if the leader wants high performance from their team.

Where the rubber meets the road ...

The dysfunctional executive team

I vividly recall being invited to facilitate a one-day team-building workshop for a senior team. It was apparent early in the workshop that two team members disliked each other intensely. There were seven members of this executive leadership team and the relationships were fine except for these two individuals. Within an hour into the workshop, these two were at each other's throats. The problem was apparent. The CEO avoided doing anything about the poor relationship between these senior officers, hoping, no doubt, that the problem would go away. Now he was hoping that my magic wand would do the trick! The final straw that had broken the camel's back was a major altercation in a team meeting one afternoon, and the eruption prompted the CEO to do some "team building." I was called in.

Now that we have defined task and people, take a moment to evaluate both dimensions of your team. How would you rate the task dimension of your team on a scale of 1 to 10 (10 is high and 1 is low)? What about the people dimension? How would you rate this dimension? What do your team members think? Do they agree with your assessment? It might be worth asking these questions of your colleagues at your next meeting together.

This assessment exercise can be a catalyst for change. A team conversation can ensue, and your team can consider ways of improving both the task and people dimensions. If nothing else, it benchmarks where team members' headspace is.

Before we venture further, I want to point out that there are two aspects to the people dimension. Team leaders must strive to build constructive one-to-one relationships with each member of their team. The team leader must also create an environment in which relationships between team members can flourish. Both aspects require focus and energy and will be elaborated on throughout this book.

Apart from taking for granted team relationships, there is another reason the people dimension is a secondary consideration after meeting the task requirements of the team. Managers are rewarded for task accomplishment. Getting the job done is what counts. The people dimension is considered less important until poor working relationships negatively affect task performance. Fostering constructive working relationships isn't rewarded. The imperative is to get the job done first and foremost. Yet we know—and have undoubtedly experienced—the unpleasant and harmful consequences of destructive working relationships. When relationships are toxic, it can blow a team to smithereens. And ultimately this results in tasks being done either poorly or not at all.

In the next chapter, we look at the research I spoke of earlier on the connection between team performance and the people dimension.

The top 10 key points

1. Team leaders have two broad responsibilities: making sure the functional tasks are completed and relationships sustained.

2. Completing tasks and encouraging good working relationships are the primary duties of a team leader.

3. The quality of team relationships is crucial to team performance.

4. The task dimension involves achieving project milestones or activities and functions the team is responsible for.

5. Until an interpersonal crisis erupts, most of the leader's energy is devoted to accomplishing the task.

6. The people dimension is commonly referred to as maintenance.

7. There are two aspects to the people dimension: one-to-one relationships between a leader and each member of the team and relationships between team members.

8. Managers are rewarded for task accomplishment.

9. Relationships are always work-in-progress.

10. When relationships are toxic, it can blow a team to smithereens.

CHAPTER 3

The three key elements of team relationships

*... how we communicate could be so much
more important to success than what we
communicate.*

*J*ack sometimes wore a Reading Football Club sweat-
shirt. *Jenny, the checkout assistant at the grocery store,
noticed it one day. "Oh," she said, "you're a Reading supporter? My team is Manchester United."*

*Normally, Jack, being shy and reserved, would have
just nodded and said something innocuous. But for some
reason, he responded with a question. "You think Man U
can beat Real Madrid next week?"*

*Jenny, with a huge smile, answered, "Oh yeah. We'll
crush them!"*

*Now, whenever Jenny sees Jack, she waves, often from
across the store. Jack often walks over, says hi, and chats
briefly about soccer.*

*That's as far as their relationship is likely to go, and
that's okay. For a couple of minutes, they surpass the normal customer/employee relationship and become two people brightening each other's day.*

And that's enough, because every relationship, however

minor and possibly fleeting, has value.

People who build great relationships treat every one of their relationships that way. That's a lesson Jack needs to take to heart more often.

In the last chapter, we discussed the two primary dimensions of team leadership: achieving tasks and building relationships. It's the people dimension that usually gets less attention. In this chapter, we consider research that indicates that the people dimension is the differentiator between great and mediocre teams. We will also consider the three key elements of the team relationships.

Sandy Pentland, director of MIT's *Human Dynamics Laboratory*, conducted some interesting research that suggests a link between task performance (the task dimension) and communication between team members (the people dimension). Further, Pentland demonstrated that it isn't the content of the conversations that makes the difference—it's the way the message is communicated. There's minimal research on communication and its connection to team performance, which is why Pentland's research is valuable.

Pentland's research confirms that communication plays a key role in team success. It's the communication patterns—more than the message—that make the difference. What's more, it's the way teams communicate in informal settings, rather than in team meetings, that counts. He suggests that

> the best predictors of productivity are a team's energy and engagement outside formal meetings.

According to Pentland's research, energy and engagement accounted for a third of the variation in dollar terms of team productivity.

Where the rubber meets the road

Why do patterns of communication matter so much?

It seems almost absurd that how we communicate could be so much more important to success than what we communicate.

Yet if we look at our evolutionary history, we can see that language is a relatively recent development and was most likely layered upon older signals that communicated dominance, interest, and emotions among humans. Today these ancient patterns of communication still shape how we make decisions and coordinate work among ourselves.

Consider how early humans may have approached problem-solving. One can imagine primitive people sitting around a campfire (as a team) making suggestions, relating observations, and indicating interest or approval with head nods, gestures, or vocal signals. If some people failed to contribute or to signal their level of interest or approval, then the group members had less information and weaker judgment, and so were more likely to go hungry.

His findings identified five key communication factors necessary for team achievement.

First, everyone in high-performing teams contributes equally in their casual interactions. One or two team members don't monopolize conversations. Second, meaningful conversations occur in face-to-face encounters with vibrance and energy. Third, team members communicate with one another without the need for the team leader to be present. Fourth, they engage in more one-on-one conversations than is usual for teams. And fifth, team members are willing to network beyond the team and bring back what they've learned to the team for its benefit. These factors illustrate the how factor in team communication.

How high-performing teams communicate flies in the face of conventional wisdom about top teams. The conventional view is that a team of experts—with superior skill sets—is the prerequisite for high performance. The All Blacks as a top sports team have a technically superior team. Although their winning ratio is impressive, they went through a slump—even with a team of skillful players. A string of relatively poor performances prompted a culture change around the mindsets of the players and how they related to one another.

Technical competence (task dimension) is a necessary part of the team performance jigsaw, but it's not the whole answer. While technical know-how is undeniably important, an underestimated success factor is the engagement patterns within the team.

A high-performing team—apart from their technical competence—has most probably mastered the communication piece (people dimension). Leadership has a major role to play in building and enabling a culture in which relationships thrive. If a leader puts sustained effort into developing the people dimension, they increase the odds of elevating team performance—assuming the necessary skill set is present. This is what the All Blacks did to turn things around.

Pentland identifies three elements critical in team dialog:

- energy
- engagement and
- exploration.

Energy is defined as the frequency and value of conversations between team members. This factor is the quality and quantity of dialog. Face-to-face conversations are usually more effective than those done via other means, recognizing that face-to-face isn't always an option. The volume of face-to-face conversations is nonetheless an important indicator of energy within a team. Lots of constructive conversations, mostly spontaneous, boost the vibe or energy of a team.

Engagement is the distribution of energy amongst team members. In high-performing teams, conversations are evenly spread between all team members—no one is isolated or excluded. One or two people don't dominate the interactions. High engagement means that everyone is in on team conversations.

This isn't as simple as it sounds. Two things must happen for everyone in a team—whether they are introvert or extrovert—to feel part of team conversations. First, each person must feel comfortable talking to everyone else in the team. For people to feel comfortable, they must feel relaxed enough to share their point of view, even when it's an unconventional contribution. Second, the person on the receiving end of these opinions must be open to a perspective that they may not necessarily agree with, at least initially. No hierarchy. No pecking order. Team engagement can be summarized as a totally collaborative environment.

Exploration—Pentland's third element—involves communication patterns beyond the team environment. In other words, these are conversations team members have with others outside the bubble of the team. Since teams don't operate in a vacuum—and are reliant on exchanging information with stakeholders within and outside the organization—alliances and associations need to be built and sustained. Building bridges with stakeholders is an important factor in proper team functioning.

In successful teams, communicating with stakeholders is shared and not left up to the leader.

In sum, conversations are critical to team success. According to Pentland:

> We now know that 35 percent of the variation in a team's performance (from their research) can be accounted for simply by the number of face-to-face exchanges amongst team members.

This raises a big question: *What can team leaders do to foster more conversations, within and beyond the boundaries of the team?* I explore this question in detail and offer many practical suggestions in PART II. So, read on!

In the next chapter, we consider team identity and how it's shaped.

The top 10 key points

1. Research indicates that the people dimension is the differentiator between great and mediocre teams.

2. Research tells us that it's the patterns of communication—more than the message—that make the difference.

3. There are five key communication factors necessary for team achievement.

4. A critical success factor in teams is the communication and engagement patterns within the team.

5. Leadership plays a major role in building and enabling a culture in which relationships thrive.

6. Three elements critical in team dialog are energy, engagement, and exploration.

7. Energy is defined as the frequency and value of conversations between team members.

8. Engagement is the distribution of energy amongst team members.

9. Exploration involves communication patterns beyond the team environment.

10. Energy and engagement account for a third of the variation in dollar terms of team productivity.

CHAPTER 4

What is team identity?

... all teams have a personality, like the people who make up the team.

Margaret was recruited to lead a newly created team of customer service officers (CSOs) in a large insurance company. She had a team of 10 people. Before she arrived, the CSOs had been working together for three months but had yet to meet as a team.

On her first day, Margaret spoke to each person in the recently formed team and explained her expectations for the CSO team. She thought this was a good start, sending a strong signal about the importance and value of teamwork.

After a week of observing the team, Margaret noticed that each CSO got their job tasks completed satisfactorily, but individuals did not seem too concerned with others in the team. This troubled her.

If someone needed help, no one seemed willing to pitch in. If a team member had a problem, nobody willingly assisted them to crack that challenge. One day Margaret observed that a CSO had an urgent personal situation to attend to and asked if someone in the team could cover for *her so she could leave early. No one offered to help, so Margaret jumped in to help at the last minute.*

Margaret felt the need to do something more about this self-centered behavior. The situation was a bad experience for everyone involved, and some of the CSOs talked about resigning or being relocated to their original team.

Time to act, thought Margaret.

She decided to get the team together for the first time in one location. If necessary, she would use Skype to make sure everyone was "present" at the meeting. Her intent was to create an environment where team members could get to know one another and discuss how they could work together in the customer service center.

Specifically, Margaret wanted to accomplish two objectives at this meeting:

- *enable time for team members to build relationships by getting to know one another on a personal level and*

- *develop processes and procedures for how the team could share work, meet the objectives of the customer service center, solve problems, resolve conflicts, and make decisions.*

Margaret thought that when the CSOs got to know each other, they'd begin to support their colleagues—they would be more conscious of their teammates.

The bottom line for Margaret was this: the CSOs needed to function as a team.

All established teams, cohorts, and groups have a unique identity. Team identity is central to the people dimension we discussed in CHAPTER 2. This identity can evolve organically, form deliberately, or be a mix of accident and design. A team's identity can be constructive or destructive, or both. Most teams possess a mix of strong and weak characteristics. Team identity can be observable or ambiguous to an observer, its members, or the leader. Despite these differences, all teams have a personality, like the people who make up the team.

In this chapter, we define team identity, what it is, and what it isn't, and introduce three functions that shape team identity. These functions can be applied purposefully and constructively to aid team performance. Or— if not attended to—these functions can form aimlessly and destructively. Either way, these three traits are the enablers of a team's identity.

The following chapter defines these three functions and their supporting characteristics. Like the functions, the characteristics can be applied intentionally—just as the New Zealand All Blacks do—to shape a positive team identity for high performance.

What is team identity?

Team identity refers to the extent to which its members identify with the team they are part of. The stronger a team's identity, the more its members connect with the team's ethos. A compelling team identity results in its members readily associating with their team before the organization at large.

This affiliation can be a positive development, provided the team identity is not too intense. Too strong a team identity builds an impenetrable barrier from the rest of the organization. A healthy identity fosters a productive culture, protecting the team from destabilizing external forces, and builds bridges with key stakeholders beyond the team. Optimal team identity offers its members a sense of purpose and belonging.

A robust team identity means its members feel loyal and obligated to the team but acknowledge and value its dependencies on outside connections. If the team's identity is too overpowering, however, the team excludes or ignores its relationships and networks outside the team. This is counterproductive.

With an excessive inward focus, the team becomes too preoccupied with itself. A disproportionately high sense of self-importance isolates the team from the rest of the organization. A "them and us" mindset is a feature of an extreme team identity.

Too much obligation, blind loyalty, and over-commitment to the team by its members are problematic. In these circumstances—where there's greater allegiance to the team than to the department that engulfs the team— it leads to uncooperative and toxic relationships with key stakeholders.

Consider this example of an unhealthy team identity.

Marco is extremely loyal to his team—a team of civil engineers in a large multi-disciplinary consulting firm. Marco is eager to meet a team priority—finishing a project report with a pressing deadline. In his haste to complete the report, he decides not to attend an important meeting with a potential client. This client wants answers to some technical questions that only an engineer can provide. Marco rationalizes his decision to neglect this meeting based on getting the "real" work of his team done. He doesn't want to "waste time" on sales calls. In frustration, the client decides to take his firm's business to a competitor.

This "loyalty" to the team can be costly. Too much identification to their team can divert a person from other organizational tasks they may perceive as less important.

But with more objective judgment, these "non-team" tasks should be considered a higher priority, such as winning new business for the organization.

Weak loyalty to the team can be counterproductive too.

A fragile team affiliation can result in a member neglecting an important team priority. For instance, Georgina, with no sense of loyalty to her team, elects to do a task for a manager in another part of the business at the expense of completing a task that is a priority in her team. Although satisfying this manager, Georgina lets her team colleagues down. A critical and urgent team task gets delayed, or worse, is overlooked. When someone's identity is not vested in their team, they can bypass its interests.

A proportional sense of team identity is vital for proper team functioning. Too much investment in a team's identity can be destructive to the rest of the organization. When imperative external commitments aren't met, or are given a disproportionately low priority, this causes problems beyond the team. And a feeble affiliation with a team can be unhelpful to the team, as I illustrated with Georgina's plight. It's a fine line—like walking a tightrope—getting the balance right between too little and too much team allegiance.

How do we know how much team loyalty is positive—or at least not negative? I'll respond to this question in CHAPTER 5.

Before we get there, let's understand team identity a little further. Team identity is not the same as team cohesion. A team can function quite cohesively without an individual's identity being vested in the team. Or, a person's loyalty can be tied to a team, even though it operates with some discord. Team identity is concerned with the allegiance a member has to their team, regardless of its unity.

There are many factors that shape a team's identity. Stand-out factors include:

- The leader's personality
- How a team member sees themselves
- What a team member enjoys doing and
- The role a team member has in the team.

Despite the many factors involved, the leader has a considerable impact on the team's identity—if they choose to exercise it.

Modern-day tribes

In *The 8 Values of Highly Productive Companies*, I claim that people are, by nature, tribal.[9] In groups of more than eight, people naturally build alliances and associations with others, in smaller clusters. In the workplace, it's common practice for people to be grouped into small work units. These clusters are formally structured around teams, sections, departments, and divisions. These structures constitute the official organizational tribes.

Apart from the prescribed organizational arrangements, informal associations and alliances develop too. People who enjoy each other's company, have associations outside work, share a common interest—such as parents with children of a similar age—are illustrations of unofficial tribes. These groups—with their own identity—form organically and are often more closely knit than the endorsed structures shown in the official organizational chart.

These tribes—whether official or unofficial—differentiate themselves consciously or sub-consciously from other tribes. They establish boundaries—like a big wire fence—that are barriers to entry, or membership. The boundaries are not always obvious at first glance—the barriers to entry can be invisible, like a force field. It could be the language the tribe uses, the attitudes they share, the thoughts they have, their mannerisms, their sense of humor, or many other things that are more subtle than a wire fence. Or it could be the proximity of their work-stations—a physical boundary. These boundaries can be social, emotional, psychological, or physical.

For example, a group of people that meets at a local café once or twice a week for lunch. This group spends their time together complaining about management. The commonly shared belief that management is incompetent and not to be trusted can be a differentiator and barrier to entry for those who believe otherwise. This clique separates itself from "outsiders" by speaking harshly of management (psychological boundary), and they meet at a café (physical boundary). Another illustration: A group of people with similar professional interests, such as a group of teachers, talk in the specific language of their profession (professional boundary). In any case, there is an exclusivity that serves to separate it from other tribes.

Formal groups in enterprises are segregated too. Teams and units are given a title and generally congregate in one office. Remote teams distinguish themselves by their projects and the way they communicate, for example. Further, these formal entities have a specific culture, based on the nature of the work they do. There are codes of conduct, rules, and work practices that are unique to their functioning as a group.

All tribes—whether formed formally or evolved

informally—protect their shared identity by the way they think and behave. Psychological boundaries aren't visible or tangible, like physical boundaries. But unseen barriers can be as restrictive and difficult to penetrate as a closed door. The group may share a certain point of view, often referred to as groupthink, or practice certain behaviors, such as being punctual or tardy. Apart from the way teams deliberate and act, physical boundaries can be doorways, buildings, or passageways. These boundaries—whatever they are—define their collective identity and prevent "outsiders" from intruding.

As I've said, a shared identity can be strong or weak. An overly resilient identity can be impenetrable to non-tribe members. For an organizational team, too strong an identity disables external relationships and alliances that sustain team success. A weak identity will cripple performance; it leaves a team open and vulnerable to having its resources cannibalized by external forces. And a brittle identity leads to suboptimal team performance. Somewhere between these extremes is the sweet spot for superior team performance.

Where the rubber meets the road

Humility is a badge of honor

Humility is deeply ingrained in Māori and broader Polynesian culture, and, indeed, the word Māori implies "normal" or "natural" to distinguish the people of the land from the gods above. To "get above yourself" is deeply frowned upon in the culture and, more broadly, in New Zealand society.

After a test match and the requisite debrief, the All Blacks do something totally unexpected.

Two of the senior players—one an international player of the year, twice—each pick up a long-handled broom and begin to sweep the player sheds. They brush the mud and gauze into small piles in the corner.

While the country is still watching replays and school kids lie in bed dreaming of All Black glory, the All Blacks themselves are tidying up after themselves.

Sweeping the sheds.

Doing it properly.

So no one else must.

Because no one looks after the All Blacks.

The All Blacks look after themselves.[10]

Three psychological boundaries of team identity

Psychological boundaries are less obvious to the observer than physical and functional boundaries; they can be created deliberately or accidentally. If psychological boundaries are attended to appropriately, they have a positive bearing on team performance. We know from research what these psychological boundaries are and their effect on the team.[11]

Being aware of these boundaries provides leaders with a useful roadmap to build a positive team identity. A team leader can therefore nurture a healthy team identity by making suitable use of these psychological boundary types. Further, there are practical strategies that can be applied by the leader to build a team identity that enables high performance to flourish.

Without concerted effort, however, these psychological boundaries take shape unintentionally and can limit the team's effectiveness. Like other boundary types, psychological boundaries can either limit or boost team performance.

The three psychological functions of team identity referred to in the literature are:

- Buffering

- Spanning and

- Bringing up boundaries.[12]

I'm going to rename two of these functions for an easier understanding of their intent and recall. Their definition and purpose remain the same as represented in the original research. I'll then offer some applied steps you can take to produce a productive team identity.

Here are my substitute descriptors:

- Buffering

- Bridging and

- Building.

Together the three "Bs" form the three functions of team identity. I will define them, explain their intent, and identify their supporting characteristics in the next chapter.

The top 10 key points

1. All established teams, cohorts, and groups have a unique identity.

2. Team identity refers to the extent to which its members identify with the team they are part of.

3. A healthy identity fosters a productive culture, protecting the team from destabilizing external forces, and builds bridges with key stakeholders beyond the team.

4. A robust team identity means its members feel loyal and obligated to the team but acknowledge and value its dependencies on outside connections.

5. A proportional sense of team identity is vital for proper team functioning.

6. Team identity is not the same as team cohesion.

7. All tribes—whether formed formally or evolved informally—protect their shared identity by the way they think and behave.

8. Too strong an identity disables external relationships and alliances that sustain team success.

9. The three psychological functions of team identity are referred to in the literature as buffering, spanning, and bringing up boundaries.

10. The substitute descriptors are buffering, bridging, and building.

CHAPTER 5
Buffering, bridging, and building

... buffering, bridging, and building—if properly exercised—serve a dual purpose; that is, to promote team identity and optimize enterprise-wide performance.

In this chapter, I will define buffering, bridging, and building—the three psychological boundary functions that shape team identity. We'll consider how these three functions work together to form identity. I'll also introduce the eight characteristics of high-performing teams that support buffering, bridging, and building.

These three functions are the building blocks for developing a high-performing team. A team leader should aim to purposely build a productive team identity, based on buffering, bridging, and building. Constructing a positive identity amplifies the people dimension of teams.

Below is an illustration of the three functions of team identity.

Figure 5.1 Three functions of team identity

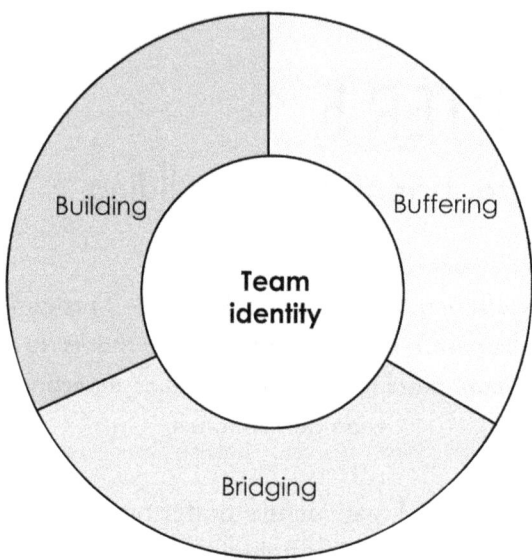

I'll elaborate on each function, starting with buffering.

Buffering

Buffering involves protecting the team's resources from unwanted outside influence, distraction, and interference. Without buffering, other teams and individuals can easily cannibalize a team's resources—whether they are human, administrative, or technical.

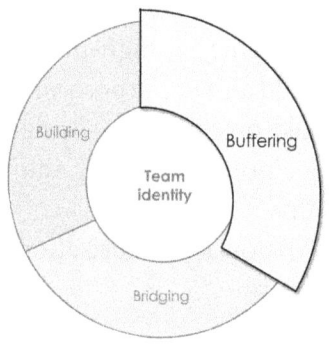

Here are some familiar examples of outside intrusions on team resources:

- A short-staffed team exerts pressure to redeploy an individual from another team to restore its capacity (human resources).

- A project manager, working in a matrix organizational structure, coaxes a functional team member to attend several time-wasting project meetings, restricting the capacity of the functional team to get its work done (human resources).

- Excessive administrative procedures suffocate a team with red tape, under the guise of accountability or transparency (administrative resources).

- A manager takes possession of what they believe is a "spare" computer to suit their team's purposes from a vacant workstation of another team (technical resources).

These common occurrences are usually justified by the perpetrator as being in the "best interests" of the organization. But even if they benefit another team or individual, these types of activities sabotage the performance of the affected team.

The impact of these outside forces can be alleviated or minimized using buffering strategies. Shielding the team from unacceptable outside disturbances involves insulating and safeguarding the team. Buffering, in other words, is anticipating these unnecessary intrusions, if possible, and appropriately defending a team's resources and strengthening its capabilities.

Unwelcome external influences can significantly dislocate a team's operations, drain its resources, or unnecessarily divert its focus. Buffering enables the team to function effectively in these situations.

Here are the three characteristics that support buffering:

- building trust

- sharing leadership and

- being agile.

I'll elaborate on these and the other characteristics in the next chapter and explain how they contribute to buffering.

When used properly, these three characteristics safeguard a team's operation from diversions and external attacks. And it's the leader's responsibility to cushion their team from outside forces that potentially disrupt its performance.

To some extent, the leader can buffer the team by planning and preparing for anticipated distractions. Buffering insulates the team and fosters a culture of self-reliance. For instance, leaders can deflect some peripheral activities that get in the way of their team's fully concentrating on its core purpose. And they can protect their resources from being depleted from outside forces. By using buffering tactics, the leader blocks, or limits, outside pressures, demands, and interferences from adversely affecting their team's efficiency and effectiveness.

Buffering tactics can, however, be overdone. Excessive buffering contributes to a perception that the team is obstructive—the leader runs the risk of being labeled an *empire builder*. These observations are unhelpful and counterproductive. But equally, it's not helpful to a team to allow undue meddling and destructive interference from others. Without some effort to buffer these inevitable peripheral forces, the team will undoubtedly compromise its effectiveness.

Buffering is based on self-interest—the self-interest of the team. But individuals and teams—to a reasonable extent—need to protect themselves from manipulation if they're to be truly successful.

Bridging

Bridging is the opposite of buffering. While buffering is an internal defense mechanism to shield the team, bridging involves reaching out to critical people and resources beyond the team. Having construc- 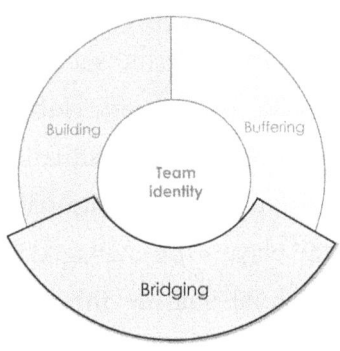 tive working relationships with key stakeholders enables the team to achieve its goals. Bridging strengthens alliances within and outside the organization. Robust business relationships and partnerships galvanize a team's relevance and raison d'être.

An obvious example of an important bridging partner is the team leader's boss. Without their support and cooperation, a team's influence diminishes, and its relevance lessens. Teams—like individuals—cannot function completely in isolation. A productive team cooperates with a variety of individuals, groups, and teams across the organization and beyond. Without collaboration and support, a team is handicapped, and its performance suffers.

Where the rubber meets the road

Sharing information with stakeholders, the key to success

New Zealand Rugby maintains an iron-clad grip on the game at all levels, including club rugby, which enables it to prioritize the success of the national team above all else. In contrast, clubs in England and France are privately owned, a situation that has, at times, led to disputes between national unions and clubs over how star players are managed and utilized. "Our system is all about sharing information between the different levels—schools, provincial and Super Rugby clubs—to ensure the All Blacks are the best and keep winning. Then we can all celebrate the victory," says Neil Sorensen, GM of New Zealand Rugby. "I doubt the Bath coach would be comfortable sitting down with the Leinster or Toulon coaches [in Europe], sharing ideas about how England could be successful on the world stage."[13]

Support and cooperation from others cannot be taken for granted—it isn't always inevitable and forthcoming. So, a stakeholder-focussed team leader paves the way by building constructive working relationships with their networks. And when there are inevitable breakdowns in communication with stakeholders, the leader tries to remedy the relationship.

Here are the two characteristics supporting bridging:

- creating purpose and
- managing stakeholders.

The leader, being the team's primary ambassador, must actively seek out outside support when and where it's needed, on behalf of their colleagues. Bridging involves building and maintaining constructive working relationships with all stakeholders.

Stakeholder management is crucial to team success. However, managing stakeholders is often bypassed or not given the priority it warrants. The probability of communication breakdowns and conflicting priorities increases without proper attention given to a team's key stakeholders. Building alliances takes time and effort; there are no shortcuts.

Buffering activities tend to get more attention than bridging. More energy is typically exerted protecting a team's resources than reaching out to vital stakeholders. Team members, therefore, need to be constantly reminded by their leaders that individual and collective accomplishment is very much dependent on the quality of relations with decision-makers within, and sometimes outside, its orbit. It only takes one soured relationship with a significant stakeholder to undermine team progress.

But bridging—like the other two functions of team identity—can be overcooked. Spending too much time networking and alliance building externally means less time buffering and building—the two internal functions of team identity.

Building

Building involves cultivating and sustaining a productive team culture. Harnessing the benefits of diversity, streamlining systems and processes, and promoting continuous learning within the team are essential building

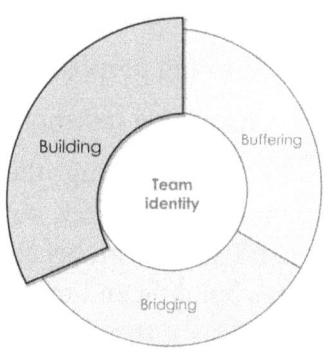

blocks of a robust team culture. Like buffering, building is internally focused. But unlike buffering—where the energy is devoted to keeping at bay external forces that might interrupt and distract the work of the team— building activities are directed to attracting the energies and enterprise of members to a common purpose. And in contrast to bridging—where the effort is directed to importing critical resources and cooperation from the wider landscape—building entails utilizing team resources to accomplish the task at hand.

Here are the three characteristics that support building:

- improving systems
- utilizing diversity and
- learning continuously.

Although represented as three distinct functions, buffering, bridging, and building are connected. For instance, being agile, a characteristic supporting buffering, aids a team's capacity to be maneuverable when sudden changes occur in its environment. As well as protecting itself from abrupt shifts in the external landscape, an agile team is better equipped to deal with its stakeholders. Being able to reach out to key stakeholders for support requires flexibility and adaptability since all stakeholder groups have their own priorities and methods of operating. Agility is also an essential ingredient of a dynamic team culture. An openness to new ways of working and adjusting rapidly are also useful characteristics of building a productive team culture. While being agile is a principle characteristic of buffering, it also assists the functions of bridging and building.

I'll further illustrate the interdependencies between the three team identity functions and their characteristics in the next chapter.

Boundary management

Leaders understandably try to eliminate or minimize restrictive boundaries in their organizations. Obstructive boundaries are barriers that stop individuals and teams from seeing beyond their immediate patch—the organization's vision is obscured. When boundaries are too dominant, team members can't see the forest for the trees. With excessive boundaries, people are not only incapable of seeing beyond their functional area, but they are not motivated to do so either. This narrow focus or tunnel vision invites a disconnect with other organizational units. In a *them and us* culture, an employee's loyalty is confined to their team. Team members in this parochial environment aren't empathetic to other tribes and their concerns, unless they "intrude" or "threaten" *their* territory. Proper boundary management counterbalances a productive team identity with an understanding of the team's enterprise-wide role.

Managers are mistaken if they believe they can eliminate psychological boundaries altogether. This isn't possible in a large, or even medium-sized, business. People, as I said in the previous chapter, are tribal by nature—boundaries naturally form in large groups, regardless of the leaders' intention or effort.

Instead of asking the question: *How can we remove boundaries altogether in the organization?* a more realistic question for managers to consider is: *Are the boundaries in the organization helpful or unhelpful?* An even better question is: *Are the organizational boundaries supporting optimal team and inter-team performance?*

These functions—buffering, bridging, and building—if properly exercised, serve a dual purpose; that is, to promote team identity and optimize enterprise-wide performance. The challenge for leaders is to balance these two objectives. Boundary management is often underdone or overdone.

If psychological boundaries are too rigid and teams too protective of their turf, they reinforce a "them and us" attitude. This uncooperative mindset isn't conducive to good inter-team communication and collaboration. And if the boundaries are too lax, people don't feel a sense of identity with their team. A weak team identity contributes to a lack of focus and ineffectiveness.

In the next chapter, we consider the Team Identity model. Supporting buffering, building, and bridging—the three functions of team identity—are the eight characteristics of high-performing teams.

The top 10 key points

1. A team leader should aim to purposely build a productive team identity, based on buffering, bridging, and building.

2. Buffering involves protecting the team's resources from unwanted outside influence, distraction, and interference.

3. The impact of these outside forces can be alleviated or minimized using buffering strategies.

4. The three characteristics supporting buffering are building trust, sharing leadership, and being agile.

5. Bridging involves reaching out to critical people and resources beyond the team.

6. Bridging strengthens alliances within and outside the organization.

7. The two characteristics supporting bridging are creating purpose and managing stakeholders.

8. Building involves cultivating and sustaining a productive team culture.

9. Harnessing the benefits of diversity, streamlining systems and processes, and promoting continuous learning within the team are essential building blocks of a robust team culture.

10. The three characteristics supporting building are improving systems, utilizing diversity, and learning continuously.

CHAPTER 6
The team identity model

... performance nose-dives without
constant attention to quality conversations
within and outside the team.

My research identifies eight characteristics of high-performing teams. There are probably other characteristics, but these eight are the most prominent. I've illustrated these eight characteristics in the Team Identity model (Figure 6.1). The model builds on the three research-based functions of team identity discussed in the previous chapter. This chapter introduces the model.

The eight characteristics of high-performing teams emphasize the people dimension of teamwork. As we covered in CHAPTER 2, effective communication and high performance go together. The aim here is to promote meaningful dialog in your team using the Team Identity model as a guiding framework.

Team communication is complex—it covers inter- and intra-team discourse. Constructive dialog within and outside the team is imperative. The importance of inter-team communication is a more apparent success factor. However, no team can perform well without developing constructive interaction with its key stakeholders, regardless of the quality of its internal communication. Both internal and external communication is required for high performance.

Conversely, performance nose-dives without constant attention to quality conversations within and outside the team. Leaders need to cultivate a culture of conversation as a foundation for success. Natural, meaningful, and frequent conversations are the cornerstone for nurturing positive working relationships.

Figure 6.1 below illustrates eight characteristics of high-performing teams.

Figure 6.1 Team identity model

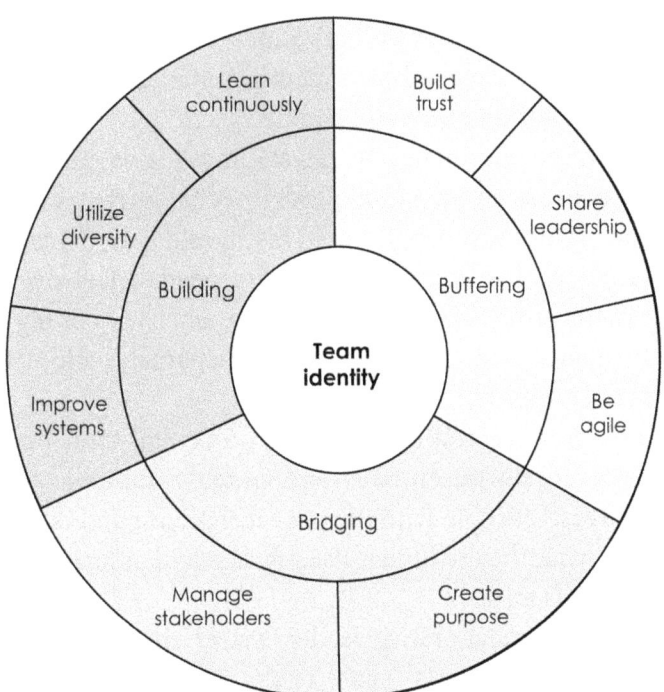

The model shows the eight [things that high-performing teams characteristically do] characteristics of high-performing teams. They are grouped to correspond with the three functions of team identity defined in the last chapter. The three characteristics of buffering—building trust, sharing leadership, and being agile—are illustrated in the lightest shade of grey. Moving clockwise around the model, the two characteristics of bridging—creating purpose and managing stakeholders—are represented in a darker shade of grey. Continuing in the same direction, improving systems, utilizing diversity, and learning continuously—the three characteristics of building—are illustrated in the darkest shade of grey.

Although the functions and characteristics of team identity are separated in the model, they are co-dependent. Each characteristic has an impact on other characteristics and functions. What's more, one characteristic can't be fully developed without other characteristics.

This is good news—and bad news …

First, the good news. By developing one of the eight characteristics in the model, it's inevitable that other characteristics will benefit too. This should reassure you. In practice, this means that leaders needn't feel overwhelmed trying to develop all the characteristics of high performance at once. Improving one characteristic will inevitably improve others.

For instance, if a team develops a crystal-clear purpose (create purpose), trust undoubtedly improves too (build trust). People with purpose feel secure and confident in what they're doing. Feeling safe and assured in a team breeds trust.

Or, if a collaborative leader shares the leadership baton with their team (share leadership), it's likely the team will be more flexible and adaptable in tackling problems and challenges (be agile). Being open and receptive to the thoughts and ideas of their colleagues, the leader draws upon different perspectives and solutions (utilize diversity). Better problem-solving potentially eventuates.

Let me share one more illustration of the interdependencies of the model. If a leader is receptive to new ways of improving the team's internal functioning (improve systems), this encourages a state of learning (learn continuously). A culture of continuous improvement becomes part of the team's fabric.

So, what's the bad news?

If one characteristic isn't fully developed, it'll adversely impact other characteristics.

For instance, if a team has generally poor working relationships with its stakeholders (manage stakeholders), this erodes trust (build trust). It then follows that low trust and adversarial stakeholder relations hinder support and will compromise a team's purpose (create purpose).

Or, if people work for an autocratic boss (no shared leadership), it narrows the range of solutions to solve problems facing the team. Drawing upon fresh perspectives is stifled (no utilizing diversity). Further, this team stops learning (no learning continuously). Groupthink prevails, growth is inhibited, and opportunities are lost.

One more. When people are expected to concentrate on their individual responsibilities—literal requirements of their job description—the team's purpose is forgotten (no creating purpose). With a fixation on their job, team members don't work as one (no shared leadership). Jobholders, with too much focus on their job, become too dependent on their leader to call the shots.

The interdependencies between the three functions of team identity and the eight supporting characteristics in the model should now be apparent.

However, unscrambling the recipe for a high-performing team into its component parts is useful for two reasons. First, it's valuable to understand the key factors of high performance. Each attribute has a role, and appreciating its contribution is helpful. And second, by identifying the necessary ingredients of high performance, the Team Identity model serves as a tool for team evaluation and development. More about that in PART III.

Here is a quick summary of the eight characteristics.

Build trust

Trust is like glue; it bonds the team together. Trust in teams can be considered in three ways: trust between leader and team members, trust between team members, and trust between team and stakeholders. Trust levels vary and fluctuate between and within these three perspectives.

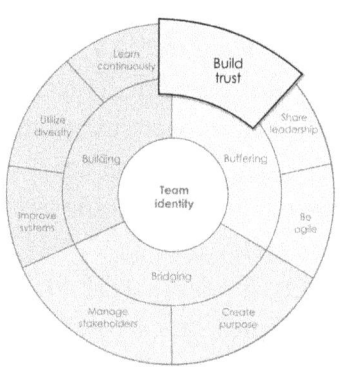

Trust is complex in the team environment. There are many relationships that exist within and outside a team. For a small team of five, including the team leader, for example, there are 10 one-on-one relationships. When one of those 10 relationships sours, it's going to affect the other nine relationships in some way. Generalizations about the trust levels of any team can be misleading.

What's more, trust ebbs and flows, depending on a

host of apparent and unclear factors. Building trust—despite its intricacies—buffers a team from outside forces, apart from other benefits. These external forces—using divide and rule tactics—can weaken or destroy team cohesion when trust is lacking.

Share leadership

Sharing leadership means working together to make decisions. Not all decisions require consultation or collaboration. For complicated problems and challenges, where there is time to deliberate, harnessing a range of perspectives in a team makes sense.

Group problem-solving and decision-making has three benefits: it exercises a wide range of opinions and perspectives, cultivates a collective commitment to a course of action, and builds cohesion. Although it takes time to consult and collaborate, shared leadership has several advantages over individual decision-making.

Shared leadership takes two forms: consultation and collaboration. Consultation is defined as the leader listening to the views and opinions of others and then deciding on a course of action. Collaboration means involving the team in a collective decision the leader will support. Both approaches enable a shared responsibility for team leadership.

A leader practicing group decision-making, where appropriate, shares the accountability for team success and failure with their team. Shared accountability strengthens team commitment. Strong commitment buffers the team from destabilizing outside influences.

Be agile

Being agile is a way of thinking and acting. Agility in practice means changing direction quickly and simply. Agility is essential for a team operating in a climate of accelerated change and uncertainty.

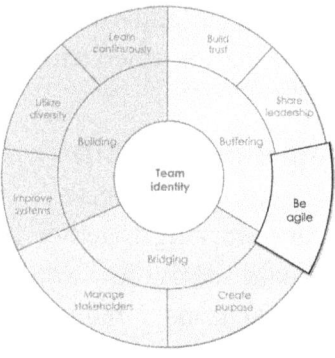

An agile team adapts rapidly and readily to new situations and circumstances. Agility is deceptively difficult to nurture, particularly in process-driven and bureaucratic organizations. Agility is nevertheless needed to survive and thrive in a changing world.

Being agile is the third characteristic supporting the buffering function of team identity. Adapting to an ever-changing landscape with maneuverability minimizes upheaval in a team. Being agile enables a team to respond to unanticipated changes in the external environment.

Create purpose

Creating and communicating a shared and clear purpose builds confidence. Since teams have myriad tasks to attend to, maintaining purpose is tough but necessary for consistent performance.

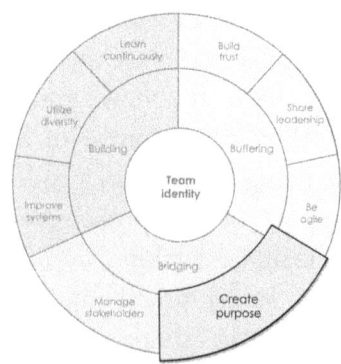

Warren Bennis, the great management guru, refers to the ability to stick to purpose as the "management of distraction."[14] A clear sense of purpose minimizes distraction and deflects disruption. A commitment to purpose means everyone in the team is on the same page.

It's not only the team that benefits from having a purpose. A clear purpose is foundational for engaging the team's stakeholders. If a team is sure about its purpose, it is reassuring to the team's stakeholders. When a team has a convincing purpose, those interacting with the team have a foundation on which to build a constructive working relationship. Clarity of purpose minimizes misunderstanding and confusion and enhances confidence in what a team can deliver.

Creating purpose supports the function of bridging. A straightforward purpose aids a team in knowing how and when to reach out to the critical people and resources necessary to support its intention.

Manage stakeholders

An often-underestimated characteristic of team success is stakeholder management. Managing stakeholders means constructively connecting with individuals and groups that have a bearing on the team's performance. It starts with a plan. A team without a plan will collide inevitably with intractable stakeholder barriers. These roadblocks limit communication channels and reduce necessary support.

And poor communication networks thwart a team's ability to get its work done. Managing stakeholders is the second essential characteristic of a team's bridging strategy.

Improve systems

Improving team systems is like renovating an old house—it never ends! New systems are added, and others are modified and renewed. House renovation is a never-ending process of rejuvenation and betterment, too. The way a team conducts its business—its systems, processes, and procedures—should always be open for constant scrutiny and enhancement.

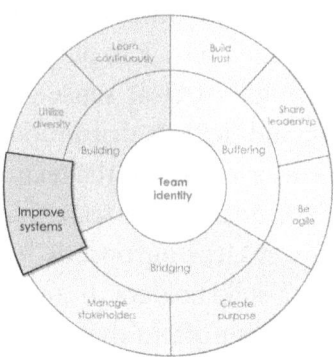

- Can a task or process be done more simply, more safely, more easily, better, or faster?

- Is a system we use useful or should it be eliminated or replaced?

are perennial questions successful teams consider.

Systems shape the team's infrastructure and its approach to getting its work done. Continually refining its systems is central to improving and sustaining team performance. Improving systems is characteristic of building a dynamic team culture.

Utilize diversity

Teams are comprised of people with varying backgrounds and experiences, differing perspectives and preferences, and multiple points of view. Harnessing

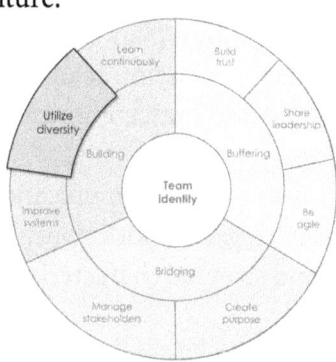

this variety to enrich team performance is finally being recognized as sensible, although, in practice, exercising diversity doesn't happen much.

Questions to ponder:

- How can the team draw upon the experience of its seasoned members?

- What are some out-of-the-box ways of thinking to solve a unique problem or dilemma the team faces?

- How can a team channel the strengths and innate talents of its people into the work that needs to be done?

By utilizing a team's diversity, a leader is exploiting the full potential of his colleagues for its benefit. This characteristic builds a culture of inclusivity by appreciating and using the inherent value people bring to the team.

Learn continuously

Learning continuously—like utilizing diversity—is a popular adage of the 21st century workplace. Learning from past successes and failures and applying these lessons in the future is a discipline of high-performing teams. Continuously learning is an attitude founded on the principle of never being satisfied with the status quo; in other words, always striving for improvement.

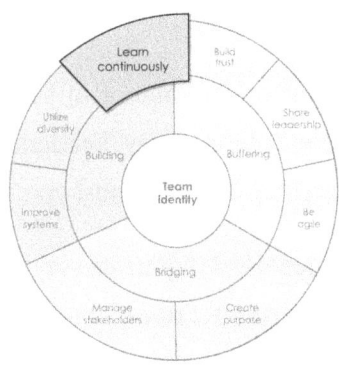

- How can we be better?

- What can we learn from this experience or project?

- How can we apply that learning in the future?

are the fundamental questions good team leaders ask to continually challenge their colleagues.

This is the third characteristic of building a go-ahead team culture.

Where the rubber meets the road

Creating a learning environment

Sean Fitzpatrick is undisputedly a great All Black, perhaps the greatest. He was capped ninety-two times, played in the 1987 Rugby World Cup winning side, and captained the side from 1992 to 1997, leading them most famously to a series win against South Africa in South Africa.

He's also a student of success; his motivational company, Front Row Leadership, is constantly busy. His message: "Be the best you can possibly be."

Success, Fitzpatrick says, is "modest improvement, consistently done." For him, it is about an unrelenting focus on the big goals—but also constant attention to the details of practice and preparation. "Business people should practice too. They should go home at night and analyse their day's performance."[15]

Shaping a team's identity

The eight characteristics we've covered shape a team's identity. In sum, the three characteristics of buffering are building trust, sharing leadership, and being agile. The two characteristics of bridging are creating purpose and managing stakeholders. And the three characteristics of building are improving systems, utilizing diversity, and learning continuously. These three functions and their supporting characteristics form team identity.

I've cited some examples of the interdependencies between characteristics across buffering, bridging, and building in the previous chapter. The links between characteristics specifically related to the functions of team identity are more apparent. I'll now briefly illustrate the interconnections of characteristics within buffering, bridging, and building.

Buffering involves preventing outside influences from cannibalizing team resources or reducing their impact. A leader prepared to share the leadership responsibility with team members (share leadership) will probably promote confidence and trust (build trust). By inviting people's opinions and involving them in the decision-making process, a leader is sharing the baton of leadership. Doing so stimulates open discussion and thinking (be agile). Sharing leadership, building trust, and being agile—all buffering characteristics—protect the team from dramatic changes in the outside world and their potentially destructive impact.

Consider the link between these three characteristics another way: If trust levels are high, the leader is going to be more comfortable consulting with team members. Heightened trust provides the leader with more confidence to involve people in decisions and sharing the leadership. This provides a foundation for agile thinking to flourish. Agility is a by-product of collaborative and consultative leadership. Being trusted, trusting, and feeling psychologically safe make enterprising decisions a more attractive option—going outside the conventional "rules" isn't so threatening.

On the other hand, a culture of distrust cripples acting with agility. Employees—constantly looking over their shoulder—naturally default to the narrow confines of their job description. The absence of trust, shared leadership, and agility makes a team vulnerable to outside attack and interference.

Bridging—with its outward rather than inward focus—involves reaching out for support to key constituencies to achieve a team's purpose. Being clear about core purpose concentrates thinking and behavior. With a strong purpose (create purpose), a team is going to be focused on delivering value to its stakeholders. In other words, a team with purpose interacts with its customers and end-users more efficiently and effectively (manage stakeholders). Constructive stakeholder management is constructing bridges with key players outside the team's sanctum.

Building, like buffering, is another internal team feature—it's essentially about cultivating and preserving a sustainable team culture. Streamlining a team's operations (improve systems) to be more useful involves attention and the capacity to learn (learn continuously). Further, upgrading a team's systems and processes relies on fresh thinking and enabling diverse thinking (utilize diversity). These characteristics—working together—build a functionally dynamic team culture.

This completes PART I. In PART II, we explore the

eight characteristics in more depth and consider some practical strategies to strengthen team identity. There are two chapters devoted to each of the eight characteristics of the Team Identity model. The first of the two chapters for each characteristic offers a detailed explanation and justification for its inclusion in the model. The subsequent chapter considers some practical tools to develop the characteristic in your team. You can begin with any characteristic, in the knowledge that by improving one aspect of the people dimension of team performance, you boost other characteristics.

In Chapter 7, we begin with building trust.

The top 10 key points

1. The three functions and eight supporting characteristics that make up the Team Identity model are interconnected.

2. Trust is a vital characteristic of any well-functioning group of people.

3. Sharing leadership in a team means working together to make decisions.

4. Agility in practice means changing direction quickly and simply.

5. Creating and communicating a shared and clear purpose builds confidence.

6. Managing stakeholders means constructively connecting with individuals and groups that have a bearing on a team's performance.

7. The way a team conducts its business—its systems, processes, and procedures—should always be open

for constant scrutiny and enhancement.

8. Utilizing a team's diversity enriches team performance.

9. Learning from past successes and failures and applying these lessons in the future is a discipline of high-performing teams.

10. The eight characteristics of high-performing teams shape a team's identity.

PART II

The eight characteristics of
high-performing teams

CHAPTER 7

Building trust

So how is trust built?
The answer: one conversation at a time.

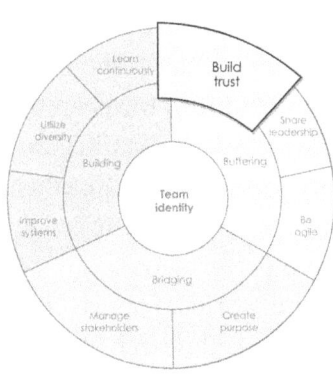

"**I**n the belly, not the back" is how Gilbert Enoka, the All Black's mental skills coach, describes the ability to deliver honest feedback. Owen Eastwood, performance coach, considers honest feedback a prerequisite of a peak-performing environment:

The key to strong peer-to-peer interaction is a high level of trust. This is trust in the sense of safe vulnerability. The leaders need to create an environment where individuals get to know each other as people and gather insight into their personal stories and working styles. This needs to be supported by the leader's role-modeling behavior around the admission of mistakes and weaknesses and fears … This is essential for safe conflict and safe confrontation, where the most important interaction often occurs.

"I think early on we didn't deal with losing very well," says Anton Oliver, a former player. "It was very much *pointing the finger, everyone very isolated. That changed a lot as the team became more collaborative, took the burden of loss equally, shared it."*[16]

Henry Ford said, "Coming together is the beginning. Keeping together is progress. Working together is success."[17] A high level of trust is characteristic of a high-performing team. Trust is the glue that makes teamwork stick.

There are countless definitions of trust. But sifting through the chaff, looking for the wheat, there are some common features in all these descriptions. American behavioral scientist James Coleman defines trust as a commitment to cooperation without certainty about the actions of trusted people.[18] Other definitions focus on the expectations of honest and trustworthy behavior. Regardless of the emphasis, trust enables people to work together. Trust permits positive social interaction—it's universally accepted as a characteristic of team performance.

High-performing teams in the world of sport—like the All Blacks—are well-documented. Research stresses the link between trust, teamwork, and performance. Trust, teamwork, and performance accord in the world of business, too. The All Blacks are a relevant and inspirational illustration of trust and its positive bearing on performance. Great teams invest in building trusting relationships. These high-performing teams also have a shared purpose. Clear purpose separates successful teams from ailing teams who don't harvest a common purpose (see CHAPTER 13).

In this chapter, we consider the core elements of trust. High trust buffers destructive outside forces from attempting to destabilize a team. Divide and rule tactics are less effective on a cohesive team that exhibits exceptional trust between its members.

Trust building isn't a one-off event. Trust is dynamic—it needs continual attention and development. It's possible, for instance, to trust someone one day and not the next. Trust can depend on the situation or circumstances. You may trust a lawyer for legal advice—but not when they proffer personal advice, for example.

Apart from the situation, trust is formed in multiple ways. Mila Hakanen and Aki Soundunsaari, in their article *Building Trust in High-Performing Teams*, contend that trust is promoted through personal knowledge, regular face-to-face interaction, empathy, respect, and genuine listening.[19] Track records and past experiences also fortify or erode trust.

Trust needs to be continually cultivated. Even a robust relationship can be tested; like a reliable car, it needs a service from time to time. Developing trust can take time, but it can be broken in the blink of an eye. Trust is a work in progress.

The five elements of trust

In one of my previous books, *Conversations at Work: Promoting a Culture of Conversation in the Changing Workplace* (co-authored with Aubrey Warren)[20], we cited five essential elements of trust:

- openness
- acceptance
- congruence
- reliability and
- competence.

These elements are experienced, communicated, and assessed through our interactions with others.

There's no doubting the central role of trust in relationships. Edelman PR has been tracking trust in government and business around the world for many years, each year releasing a "trust barometer."

> We believe trust is an asset that enterprises must understand and properly manage in order to be successful in today's complex operating environment. Unlike reputation, which is based on an aggregate of past experiences with a company or brand, trust is a forward-facing metric of stakeholder expectation.[21]

In his book *The Speed of Trust*, Stephen M.R. Covey makes the case for investing in trust relationships with his equation that when trust goes up, speed goes up and cost goes down. And when trust goes down, speed goes down and cost goes up.[22] Or, as Ralph Waldo Emerson put it, "our distrust is very expensive."

So how is trust built? The answer: one conversation at a time. In CHAPTER 3 we discussed the relevance of quality interaction in teams and its connection to performance. So let's look at the five elements of trust, briefly, and its application to team conversations.

Appropriate *openness* in our conversations gives others a sense of our self-confidence and willingness to connect with them. Being a closed book or playing your cards close to the chest means it's hard to know what you are really like. Building trust involves some openness or self-disclosure. Yes, there's a risk of rejection in being an open book—but trusting someone is ultimately about candidness and understanding.

Some people are naturally more open about themselves than others (which is not always a good thing—
especially if you're seated next to them on a long flight!).
But any healthy relationship grows from being appropriately self-disclosing. Openness communicates to the
other person a willingness to invest in the bond. We can't
expect others to let us know about themselves if we aren't
willing to do the same. Leaders need to take the first step
in being suitably open with those whom they lead.

Acceptance is the flipside of the openness coin. When
people share information about themselves, they've
chosen to take a risk—to be a little vulnerable. We
know there's the chance of rejection or judgment when
we divulge something personal about ourselves, so it's
important that we manage our prejudices and biases to
accept others for who they are and accept their perspectives as their own, even if we don't agree.

Congruence in communication is measured by how
aligned our words are with what we mean. Do we talk
straight, or do we couch our opinions and contributions
in qualifications or hesitant phrases? There's a balance to
be struck here, of course, between bluntness and avoidance. We can trust people who are direct a lot more than
those who always try to make things *nice* by avoiding the
hard issues. But bluntness also has its limitations. The
straight language people use is often stronger than the
actions they're prepared to take—which is incongruent
rather than congruent.

Congruence means being assertive—that balance
between aggressiveness and avoidance. It involves an element of trust because it communicates respect—respect
for our own views and respect for the capacity of others

to handle reasonable directness.

Reliability is a familiar element of trust—it sends a message that you will do what you say you will do. Over-promising, under-delivering, procrastinating, and inconsistency signal a lack of reliability—and result in erosion of trust.

And finally, *competence* is an element of trust that's sometimes overlooked. We all learn to trust ourselves and others in some situations but not others, as I mentioned before. We may trust our own judgment in financial matters, based on our expertise in that area, but not trust ourselves to make strategic decisions because we acknowledge our limitations there. Likewise, we may trust our manager to competently lead a project but not to make a presentation about it to stakeholders. Trust and distrust can be associated with task competence and incompetence. Because physical, emotional, and professional safety is fundamental to us, we instinctively look for demonstrated competence as a part of our trust assessment.

These five elements of trust—openness, acceptance, congruence, reliability, and competence—increase or reduce trust in our relationships. It's helpful to consciously exercise them when communicating with others.

Where the rubber meets the road

Growing trust in your working relationships

Nan Russell writes about trust as "the new workplace currency" in a 2013 Psychology Today article. Relationships that enable trust and bring exceptional results don't happen unless there's a conscious intention to make them happen. That intention starts with common sense approaches around basic relationship building.

Trust grows in relationships when …

The relationship is mutually beneficial.

You bring the best of who you are into the relationship; the best includes core elements like integrity, tolerance, honesty, and trustworthiness.

You want the best for the other person.

The relationship is more important than any single outcome. You invest time, communication, commitment, and authenticity.

You show genuine care, concern, and compassion.

You operate with appreciation, politeness, and inclusion.

You give more than you take, while keeping your interests in view.

You help others achieve their aspirations, dreams, goals, or personal best.

You respect where others are coming from—their knowledge, experience, state of mind, values, beliefs, and needs.

> Trust may be at historic lows, but so what? Trust is a local issue. If you want more trust in your work relationships, start with yourself. A practice of trust-building is a practice of relationship-building. If you want to grow trust or rebuild broken trust, focus on building your relationships.[23]

Here are some additional pointers for leaders to cultivate a culture of trust within their team, suggested by *MindTools*.[24]

Lead by example

Start by setting the tone through your example. Show your team members you trust them. Begin from a position of trusting your colleagues, boss, and stakeholders. I acknowledge that's not always easy, or possible. But remember what Frank Crane, American minister and author, said: "You may be deceived if you trust too much, but you will live in torment if you don't trust enough."[25] We should never forget that the people are always watching and taking cues from us—take the opportunity to show them what trust in others really looks like.

If you manage a virtual team, aim to treat your team members just as you would if they were working beside you. For starters, make every effort to be on time for conference calls or video chats and let your remote team members know when you'll be absent or unavailable.

Most of all, follow through on the promises you make. Keeping promises is imperative in a virtual team arrangement because your word is often all you can give.

Following through forms trust immediately, raises team morale, and sets expectations.

Communicate openly

Open communication is essential for creating trust, as stated previously. You want everyone in your team talking to one another in an honest, meaningful way, and this can be accomplished in several ways.

Here are four simple suggestions.

First, form a Team Values Charter to define the way team members should interact with one another. We cover this powerful tool in the next chapter.

Second, be prepared to organize some team-building exercises so that team members can get to know each other beyond a superficial level. When planned well, these activities break the ice and encourage people to open up and start communicating in the early stages of team formation. For well-established teams, these team development experiences offer insights into the way people prefer to operate in teams. It's instructive to acknowledge that other people's practices and predilections are as valid as your own (see CHAPTERS 19 & 20).

Third, if you're not doing this already, meet regularly, so that all team members have a chance to talk about their progress and air any grievances they have. These meetings should be a vehicle for open communication. It's also an opportunity for team members to talk, get to know each other, support one another, solve problems collaboratively, and share leadership (see CHAPTER 9).

And finally, make sure that you walk the talk. Whenever you have important or relevant information to share, do so as soon as possible. Demonstrate that open communication is valued by being transparent with your team. The more you share with your team members— proving that you don't have a hidden agenda—the easier they'll feel trusting you.

Get to know team members

It's helpful to remind yourself that your team members are people. Think about organizing social occasions that help team members to share their personal stories and bond. In one-on-one interactions, ask about family, interests, and hobbies, sensitively and genuinely. Start these conversations by sharing some personal information about yourself—be prepared to self-disclose. Socialize after work or at lunch—don't overdo it, though. But socializing occasionally builds relationships and affirms the people dimension of teamwork.

If your team works remotely and it is newly formed, schedule an online meet and greet to help members get to know one another as individuals. Ask everyone to write a paragraph or two in their online profiles about their expertise and skills, personal history, and interests. And use chat or instant messaging applications to keep the lines of communication alive.

Discourage the blame game

When people work together, mistakes and disappointments inevitably occur, and it's easy to point the finger of blame. However, when everyone starts apportioning blame, an unpleasant atmosphere rapidly arises, lowers morale, undermines trust, and reduces productivity. These are all symptoms of playing the blame game.

Instead, encourage everyone in the team to think

about the blunder in a constructive way. *What can we do to fix what happened and move forward together?* And *How can you make sure that this mistake doesn't happen again?* are the questions to ask.

Discourage cliques

Cliques can form within a team, often between team members who share common interests, perspectives, or work tasks. These alliances can erect unhelpful psychological barriers and make others outside the clique feel isolated. This is the inherent human tribalism I discussed in CHAPTER 5. Unnecessary and unhelpful tribes or cliques undermine trust.

Get on the front foot and have an open discussion about the negative effect of cliques with your team, preferably before they have a chance to form. Listen to what people think about cliques and their consequences. Only by addressing this cooperatively can you discourage negative tribalism within the team.

Discuss trust issues

If you manage an established team with low levels of trust, it's essential to find its origin so that a constructive remedy can be found. Don't sweep it under the carpet—it won't go away unless it's addressed.

Consider giving your team a simple questionnaire to complete anonymously. Invite team members to rate the level of trust in the team on a scale of 1 to 10 (10 being high and 1 being low) and give their reasons. Once you've read their responses, bring everyone together to talk about the results, making sure you respect people's anonymity. This works wonders in most cases.

In the next chapter, we discuss the Team Values Charter—a great tool for trust-building.

The top 10 key points

1. Trust can be defined as a commitment to cooperation without certainty about the actions of trusted people.

2. High trust buffers destructive outside forces from attempting to destabilize a team.

3. Research stresses the link between trust, teamwork, and performance.

4. There are five essential elements of trust: openness, acceptance, congruence, reliability, and competence.

5. Lead by example.

6. Open communication is essential for creating trust.

7. Get to know team members personally.

8. Don't encourage the blame game.

9. Discourage cliques.

10. Discuss trust issues.

CHAPTER 8

Forming a team values charter

> Talent can't paper over the cracks of mistrust in a team. It doesn't matter how capable or talented people are, the team won't reach its full potential if reasonable trust isn't present.

Imagine a situation where two people sit side by side in their team environment for 10 years without uttering one word to each other—not even a hello, good morning, how are you? Not one word!

Well, it happened.

I was consulting to an internationally recognized orchestra. Two musicians, who sit side by side on stage in the concert hall and in rehearsal, refused to speak with one another for a decade.

When they were compelled to communicate one-to-one about artistic matters, they'd write notes and pass them to each other, without making so much as eye contact.

After sitting down with the musicians separately in a coaching session, I was told of a relatively trivial incident that had occurred between the two artists early in their *career in the orchestra. Although a minor matter, a violation of trust resulted from that encounter, and they decided not to speak to each other for what amounted to thousands of rehearsals, orchestral meetings, and concerts.*

Their long-standing spat created tension in the section and ultimately across the orchestra, comprising nearly 100 musicians. The section principal didn't know what to do and eventually gave up trying to reconcile their differences.

I met with the two musicians separately again to discuss this breach of trust. After giving both combatants a good hearing, I suggested they meet over coffee and talk without anyone else present. I organized this and set up the meeting.

After some ducking and weaving, they did finally, reluctantly meet. To their pleasant surprise—and to the relief of the entire orchestra and its management—the meeting resulted in their ironing out their differences. They agreed to work more closely together and have been happily communicating with each other ever since. The performance of the orchestra has improved appreciably, not to mention the boost in morale.

Talent can't paper over the cracks of mistrust in a team. It doesn't matter how capable or talented people are, the team won't reach its full potential if reasonable trust isn't present.

What about the other way around; that is, a team with high trust and low capability? At least with elevated trust, there's a possibility of the team attaining a reasonable level of performance, despite limited potential. When trust is present, each person can thrive, and collectively, the team can reach its narrow capacity. So, trust is a critical factor in determining an individual and team's capacity, whatever that may be.

Heightened trust is characterized by people willingly sharing important information; they go out of their way to support each other and rise to meet the expectations of their colleagues. People working in a cohesive team feel obligated to develop their capabilities—they don't want to let each other down. When people trust one another, the group becomes a team—they commit to a shared purpose and mutual obligation.

In the previous chapter, I explained how the leader can create a trusting environment. In this chapter, we'll look at the Team Values Charter—a great tool for promoting trust.

I repeat, trust is an essential characteristic of an effective and well-functioning team. Trust is like the mortar that holds a brick wall together. Trust provides psychological safety—one of the foundational human requirements psychologist Abraham Maslow identifies in his *Hierarchy of Needs*. When people feel secure in the company of those they work with, they feel comfortable about opening up, taking suitable risks, and exposing their vulnerabilities.

Distrust, on the other hand, leads to behavior such as following the procedures manual to the letter, minimal fresh thinking and new ideas, limited cooperation and no collaboration, and reduced performance, to name a few obvious symptoms. People operating in a no-trust environment spend their time protecting themselves and their interests—time that should be spent supporting one another to accomplish the team's purpose.

Trust is the fuel that drives knowledge sharing. Several studies show a link between trust and knowledge acquisition.[26] If team members trust one another, it stands to reason that they are more likely to share their knowledge and communicate more frequently and openly.

Where the rubber meets the road

"The First XV"

Here is The First XV—15 All Black principles, based on the team's being 15 players working together towards a common purpose – to win a game of rugby.

1. Sweep the sheds
Never be too big to do the small things that need to be done.

2. Go for the gap
When you're on top of your game, change your game.

3. Play with purpose
Ask "why?"

4. Pass the ball
Leaders create leaders.

5. Create a learning environment
Leaders are teachers.

6. No obnoxiousness
Follow the spearhead.

7. Embrace expectations
Aim for the highest cloud.

8. Train to win
Practice under pressure.

9. Keep a blue head
Control your attention.

10. Know thyself
Keep it real.

> **11. Sacrifice**
> *Find something you would die for and give your life to it.*
> **12. Invent your own language**
> *Sing your world into existence.*
> **13. Ritualize to actualize**
> *Create a culture.*
> **14. Be a good ancestor**
> *Plant trees you'll never see.*
> **15. Write Your legacy**
> *This is your time.*[27]

A Team Values Charter is a trust-building tool to help a team to work together in a mutually agreed way. It's not time-consuming, but it can be very insightful and effective. The Team Values Charter is best done face-to-face with all team members present, but it can be done remotely if necessary.

Here's how it works.

At the beginning of a meeting, ask each person in the team to respond in writing to five questions. You want your team to have thought clearly and deeply about the questions—writing answers helps the thinking process. This isn't an exercise that should be done off the cuff. And as the team leader, it's imperative that you participate in the exercise too.

Here are the five questions:

1. *What* one value is important to you when working as part of this team?

2. *How* do you define your value?

3. *Why* is this value important to you?

4. *What* types of behaviors violate this value?

5. *What* types of behaviors are consistent with your value?

To illustrate, here are my responses to the five questions:

1. *What* one value is important to you when working as part of this team?

    a. Respect.

2. *How* do you define your value?

    a. Respect to me means being prepared to listen to another point of view from a team member in an open and non-judgmental way, even if you don't necessarily agree with their perspective.

3. Why is this value important to you?

    a. This value of respect is important to me because I believe we ought to be encouraging diversity in the way we think and operate as a team. And if we are prepared to respect the views of others that we don't necessarily agree with, it will encourage others to speak up.

4. *What* types of behaviors violate this value?

    a. I think someone interrupting another colleague before they have finished fully expressing their point of view is inappropriate. In my mind, this is disrespectful.

5. *What* types of behaviors are consistent with your value?

    a. Actively listening to a different point of view with respect and interest.

After everyone has completed their written responses, you invite each of your colleagues to share their responses to the five questions with the rest of the team. It's a good idea for you to start the conversation by verbalizing your responses—this sets an inclusive tone.

As each team member is offering their perspective, encourage colleagues to ask questions of the presenter for clarification or makes constructive comments. This exercise should be interactive and not a series of static presentations. The more dialog and informality in the room the better.

Once everyone has shared their responses to these five questions, the team has effectively captured the content necessary to create a Team Values Charter. If there are six members in the team including the team leader, and each person has chosen a different value, the team values charter will consist of six values and a defining statement for each value.

The defining statement of each value should come from the team member's response to the second question: *How do you define your value?* The reply to this question is the originator's meaning of their key value.

For example, consider my value: *Respect*. Respect can mean many different things. It can mean anything from showing basic courtesy to treating people as equals to deferring to another's judgment. In my illustration, respect is a preparedness to listen to others in an open and non-judgmental way. So, it's appropriate that this response is captured in the charter to reflect my perspective of that value.

If more than one person has the same value, then two or more team members work together to come up with a defining statement that captures their collective thoughts on that value.

For example, a person defines *respect as listening to others* and another defines respect as treating people courteously. A combined statement might read: *To listen to others and be courteous to colleagues.* The key is that everyone in the team has input into the composition of the charter.

When the wording in the definition of the value is clear and reflects the sentiments of the contributing team member(s), the Team Values Charter can be framed and put on the wall of the regular meeting room. The charter can also be distributed and displayed prominently on the desktops of the six team members as a reminder of their agreement to each other.

As you can see, this exercise is straightforward. But don't be fooled by its simplicity—it's enormously potent. The team members will be emotionally connected to their charter because a value they strongly believe in is part of it. In other words, team members genuinely own the charter.

And because of this strong sense of ownership, team members are much more likely to adhere to it. You may find that from time to time members of the team hold each other accountable to the charter. This is, of course, a welcome development.

From a leadership perspective, you now have a tool that expands your influence beyond the task dimension. How so? You too can—and should—hold the team (and yourself) accountable to your charter. The charter is a shared vision of how the team wants to work together. By applying this tool, the leader has effortlessly led the team to design their own determination of how they see themselves operating as a team. The team has also provided you with a set of values to which to hold each of you accountable for your behavior and actions. This exercise develops the people dimension of your team.

The Team Values Charter builds trust by creating a framework that people believe in and honor.

When a new member joins the team, invite them to contribute their value and associated definition. The charter is then updated to include their value and meaning. If this person is replacing someone in the team, leave the previous team member's value in the charter. This sends a signal to the remaining members that their contribution will outlive their involvement in the team.

Apart from holding the team accountable to a set of values, the Team Values Charter provides another avenue for reviewing performance—the way people work together. You can observe the tasks and activities of the team (task dimension) through the prism of a set of collective values. *Was that behavior consistent with our charter? Did we stay true to our charter throughout the project?* are questions you should ask and assess the team against.

Team members will also be able to evaluate the way they work individually and collectively via their values—they are able to hold themselves answerable to the charter as well.

The charter works for a basic but compelling reason—people don't argue with their own data! They own the charter and will likely uphold its values, or at least realize when a value has been infringed. The charter builds trust, augments the people dimension of teamwork, and buffers the team against destabilizing external influences.

In the next chapter, we consider the characteristic of shared leadership—another means of protecting the team from outside forces.

The top 10 key points

1. Heightened trust is characterized by people willingly sharing important information; they go out of their way to support each other and rise to meet the expectations of their colleagues.

2. Trust is an essential characteristic of an effective and well-functioning team.

3. Trust is the fuel that drives knowledge sharing.

4. The team values charter is based on five questions.

5. Once everyone has shared their responses to these five questions, the team has effectively captured the content necessary to create a team values charter.

6. When the wording in the definition of the value is clear and reflects the sentiments of the contributing team member(s), the team values charter can be framed and put on the wall of the regular meeting room.

7. Because of this sense of ownership, team members are much more likely to adhere to it.

8. By applying this tool, the leader has effortlessly led the team to design their own determination of how they see themselves operating as a team.

9. The team values charter builds trust by creating a framework that people believe in and honor.

10. The charter builds trust, augments the people dimension of teamwork, and buffers the team against destabilizing external influences.

CHAPTER 9
Sharing leadership

Dispersing leadership amongst all members helps bolster the team in a climate of accelerated change and uncertainty.

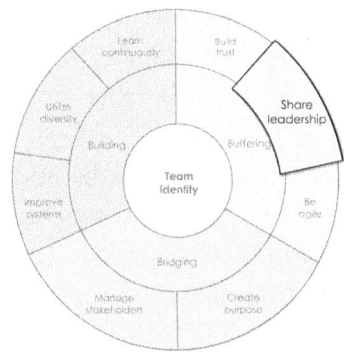

Leadership isn't the sole province of any one player in the All Blacks. Instead, the New Zealand team considers themselves to be one captain and 15 leaders.

Everyone has a turn to speak, offering an equal voice and equivalent contribution to the team. The All Black organization trusts their players to do what needs to be done, and so their members become leaders, rising to the occasion and proving they're worthy of that trust.

There's no concern when senior All Blacks retire—the younger crop of leaders is already capable of taking over the responsibilities of mentoring the newer members and carrying on the team legacy. When the big moment arrives, every team member can confidently stand up and lead their team to victory.[28]

Global expansion, the rate and pace of industry

restructuring, and the relentless number of mergers and acquisitions require a new style of leadership. Agility, flexibility, and maneuverability are the success factors in an unstable environment. Shared leadership is the right approach to meet these turbulent times. Tapping into the full range of insights, skills, and abilities in a team is what shared leadership promises. Dispersing leadership amongst all members helps bolster the team in a climate of accelerated change and uncertainty.

Management guru Marshall Goldsmith defines shared leadership as maximizing the team's capabilities by enabling individuals to contribute their expertise.[29] The leadership responsibility can be managed straight-forwardly by one person in a stable and predictable environment. But unilateral leadership isn't suitable when confronting an ever-changing and unpredictable environment.

Sharing the leadership means using the skills and talents of all team members, wherever and whenever possible. Further, shared leadership disseminates power, authority, and decision-making widely and deeply across the team.

Shared leadership is like the conducting of an orchestra. A conductor leads, using their body language—they bring in and exit out sections of the orchestra with precise timing to create a piece of music. The conductor doesn't play an instrument. Armed with a baton or using hand gestures—with accompanying facial expressions—the conductor's role is to draw upon the diverse sounds of the instruments and players in the orchestra. The conductor is shared power personified.

Where the rubber meets the road

Perspectives on shared leadership

A leader is best when people barely know he exists, when his work is done, his aim fulfilled, they will say we did it ourselves—Lao Tzu

You manage things; you lead people—Rear Admiral Grace Murray Hopper

The first responsibility of a leader is to define reality. The last is to say thank you. In between, the leader is a servant—Max DePree

Before you are a leader, success is all about growing yourself. When you become a leader, success is all about growing others—Jack Welch

My own definition of leadership is this: The capacity and the will to rally men and women to a common purpose and the character which inspires confidence—General Montgomery

Never doubt that a small group of thoughtful, concerned citizens can change the world. Indeed, it is the only thing that ever has—Margaret Mead

To command is to serve, nothing more and nothing less—Andre Malraux

I start with the premise that the function of leadership is to produce more leaders, not more followers—Ralph Nader

A great person attracts great people and knows how to hold them together—Johann Wolfgang Von Goethe

When I give a minister an order, I leave it to him to find the means to carry it out—Napoleon Bonaparte

Outstanding leaders go out of their way to boost the self-esteem of their personnel. If people believe in themselves, it's amazing what they can accomplish—Sam Walton

No man will make a great leader who wants to do it all himself, or to get all the credit for doing it—Andrew Carnegie

Leadership is the art of getting someone else to do something you want done because he wants to do it—General Dwight Eisenhower

Never tell people how to do things. Tell them what to do and they will surprise you with their ingenuity—General George Patton

As we look ahead into the next century, leaders will be those who empower others—Bill Gates

For a leader to share power, they must be prepared to think and act in certain ways. Here are some suggestions you can use to share leadership and maximize the talents of your team.

Give away power

Giving away power to the most qualified or capable individuals in a team makes sense. This includes delegating functional and non-functional tasks. Functional tasks relate to the work activities of the team. If team members have tightly defined job boundaries or specifications—which is unfortunately too often the case—it can be challenging to encourage others to share roles. In these circumstances, it may seem like intruding on the territory of others.

Under tightly structured functional task allocations, jobholders inevitably view the tasks listed in the job description as their territory. A team member with a job specification will, at best, reluctantly relinquish these tasks to others. Protective and territorial behavior can thwart the sharing of tasks.

For example, a Key Result Area (KRA)—explicitly stated in Tom's job description—is "administration." Tom is the designated administration officer in the team. An administrative task is framing the team budget. Despite budgeting being part of Tom's job description, Brooke, the team leader, wants to delegate this task to someone else in the team. Brooke feels that Felicity, another member of the team—who doesn't have budgeting listed in her job description—is better equipped to formulate a budget. Delegating budgeting to Felicity—which makes perfect sense to Brooke—causes friction in the team, with Tom feeling threatened that his territory has been encroached on. The temptation in these circumstances is for the team leader to soldier on and leave this responsibility with Tom, despite his having inferior budgeting capabilities.

The problem with clearly defined job specifications—aside from territorial challenges—is that they don't always suit the talents and capabilities of the jobholder. The solution is to loosen these job specifications by adopting a multiskilling strategy. Multiskilling means everyone in a team is equipped and expected to carry out several tasks beyond the narrow confines of their job description. We cover the application of multiskilling in the next chapter.

Non-functional activities are usually less clearly defined and not embedded in the job specification. They include aptitudes such as:

- negotiation
- strategic planning
- interpersonal communication
- promoting to a wider audience
- project organization

These non-functional activities are best assigned to those who have a natural talent for them. In CHAPTER 20, we cover non-functional attributes and how they can be used for the benefit of the team.

Redefining the limits of decision-making power

Redefining the bounds of decision-making power refers to the extent and limits of authority a team member may exercise. Attending to decision-making authority is particularly relevant when working "outside" one's stated KRAs. If trust levels are healthy and good communication channels established, people will feel safer in exercising their discretionary decision-making power. Understanding one's limits of authority is achieved through frequent and purposeful conversations between leader and team members and between team members.

Communication is to shared leadership as oil is to a motor mower—neither functions without regular conversations or oil top-ups, respectively. As discussed in CHAPTER 7, communication and trust are inseparable. By establishing trust, people feel free to communicate amenably. And by communicating openly, trust increases.

Stimulating a climate of enterprise

Do I play it safe or show initiative (take a risk)? is a question people often grapple with silently at work. Plus, when given a choice between following the "system" and displaying initiative, it's usual for people to take the *safe* route. The safe route could be deferring upward, following standard operating procedures, or sticking to a tried and proven path. But having a solution-focused mindset means going against the grain occasionally and exhibiting enterprise and free thinking. Promoting prudent enterprising behavior, when necessary, enables others to back themselves and show initiative.

All decisions at work—or anywhere in life—can follow three pathways. Some decisions require original thinking and novel approaches. In extraordinary circumstances, such as handling a unique customer request, the leader expects team members to display initiative. Other decisions are best made using a standard and prescribed approach. In safety situations, for example, a leader expects team members to *follow the rules*; in other words, to adhere to standard workplace procedures. And other decisions can be made by choosing either enterprising behavior or following protocol. In these instances, if a leader restrains enterprising behavior, people are probably going to default to the safe path—even though showing some initiative may be the better option.

Here is a constructive conversation you can have with the whole team to promote enterprising behavior. Draw three columns on a large whiteboard. Label the left-hand column *procedural*. Label the middle column as *procedural or resourceful*. And mark the right-hand column *resourceful*. Then invite your team to identify decisions they make that are procedural; that is, they must be done by the book. Record them in the left-hand column.

Now go to the right-hand column and ask the team to think of decisions that can be made with independent thought, namely, resourceful. You might need to provide an example of resourcefulness, particularly in a heavily regulated work setting. Again, record their responses.

Now identify decisions that can be made either procedurally or resourcefully and record them in the middle column. Ask for examples. Discuss these decisions. *Can these decisions in the future be best made following a procedure or by independent judgment?* Perhaps it will depend on the situation. This discussion can offer some psychological safety for team members to exercise their independent thought in appropriate circumstances.

Give people autonomy

Giving people the freedom to prioritize their tasks and complete their work how they choose to, is difficult for some leaders. When the leader is a technical expert, it can be hard not to interfere in the work of others. It's tough for the technically proficient leader to bite their tongue and not intervene in the work of others. But sharing the leadership demands letting go and trusting others to get the job done.

Dan Pink in his great book *Drive: The Surprising Truth About What Motivates Us* argues that knowledge workers need three things to perform: *autonomy*, *mastery*, and *purpose*.[30] Autonomy is having the freedom to make decisions about the way one tackles a task or project. Mastery is technical know-how that comes from skills development. And understanding purpose is what Simon Sinek refers to as the "why." *Why is this job or task important?* In other words, purpose is understanding a task's relevance to the team's overall purpose. Granting team members some autonomy in doing their work boosts motivation.

Don't second-guess people

When a leader doesn't give people the freedom and autonomy to make their own decisions, it sends several bad messages. A micromanaged employee will take this in at least one of three ways:

- my boss doesn't trust me
- my boss doesn't think I know what I'm doing or
- my boss thinks they know best.

Most likely, being micromanaged will be interpreted in all three ways!

Trust your team. Trust that people will do their best and do the right thing. Even if you know best, questioning people's motives is unhelpful. Second-guessing people is the quickest way to make them assume you have no confidence in them.

The solution to micromanaging is communication. Meet and explain your expectations at the beginning of a project. Set up opportunities throughout the project to discuss progress. These routine work-in-progress meetings are an opportunity to oversee progress (or lack of progress). If done sensitively and respectfully, these check-ins won't be viewed by team members as being intrusive.

The leader as coach

Good coaches help others to help themselves. Teach people how to catch a fish rather than catching the fish for them. Capable coaches ask questions—they encourage others to think and solve their own problems.

John Whitmore introduced us to the G.R.O.W. coaching model. GROW helps the coachee to think through a way to resolve a problem. G stands for *goal.*

- What are you trying to achieve?

- What is the result you are looking for?

- How will you know you are successful?

are good questions to help the other person identify the ideal outcome.

R represents *reality.*

- What are the barriers that are likely to get in the way?

- What are some of the main challenges you are likely to face?

- Is there anything that will prevent you from achieving that goal?

are relevant questions to help the other person consider the potential obstacles and barriers.

O stands for *options.*

- What options have you considered?
- What are the various ways you intend to get this done?
- Have you considered the best way forward?

are questions that assist the other person to consider the ways of getting the job done.

And W represents *what's next?*

- What do you need to do straight away to get the ball rolling?
- What support do you need?
- What can I do to help?

are questions to get the coachee into action.

GROW is easy to use and is based on sharing the leadership. Try it out.

Growth and development

Research proves there is a connection between shared leadership and team learning.[31] The more a team has responsibility for team performance, the more it learns and grows. Sharing the team leadership baton builds human capacity, individually and collectively. Growth comes in the form of continuous improvement from reflective practice.

Shared leadership has another bonus for the leader—it frees up their time. Delegating and challenging others to take up more responsibility gives the leader the time to coach and develop others. Team members become partners, not subordinates.

In the next chapter, we consider the implementation of a *Skills Matrix* to build capacity and share leadership.

The top 10 key points

1. Shared leadership is defined as maximizing all the team's capabilities by enabling individuals to contribute their expertise.

2. Giving away power to the most qualified or capable individuals in a team makes sense.

3. Redefining the bounds of decision-making power refers to the extent and limits of authority a team member can exercise.

4. All decisions at work—or anywhere in life—can follow three pathways.

5. Promoting prudent enterprising behavior, when necessary, enables others to back themselves and show initiative.

6. Sharing the leadership demands letting go and trusting others to get the job done.

7. When a leader doesn't give people the freedom and autonomy to make their own decisions, it sends several bad messages.

8. Leaders need to see themselves as coaches rather than managers.

9. The antidote for feeling second-guessed is for the leader to meet and explain their expectations at the outset of a project.

10. Research proves there is a connection between shared leadership and team learning.

CHAPTER 10
Designing a skills matrix

The goal is to have everyone competent in all shared team tasks.

When I finished school as a baby boomer, my parents encouraged me to consider a specialized occupation for job security. Their reasoning was well-intended, simple, but as it turns out, misguided. If you can find a niche where you can specialize, you're guaranteed employment and a secure job. This popular assumption was predicated on a stable and relatively predictable pre-globalized marketplace. The logic of my parents' argument no longer applies—the rules have fundamentally changed.

I vividly recall a conversation with my father about my career options in my senior year of school. At the time, I had no idea of what I wanted to do with my life. Although I was more interested in humanities than sciences, my father suggested I consider optometry.

"Optometry is a specialized area. People will always need glasses and you'll be secure in that field," Dad said, with conviction. "You need to find a specialty—something that's secure and will be around forever. At some stage in everyone's life, they'll need glasses."

My father's argument made sense at the time. However, I wasn't excited by the thought of working in the field of vision care. Optical laser surgery became possible a decade after our conversation. Many people now have the option of correcting their eyesight by surgery, instead of purchasing a set of spectacles or contact lenses. It's little wonder, then, that optometrists are diversifying into other areas, such as selling sunglasses.

A specialized profession with a seemingly secure future is not quite as sheltered as it once was. As in most professions and occupations, diversification is the new reality.

In the previous chapter, we defined shared leadership and its contribution to team performance. Sharing the leadership buffers a team in a rapidly changing world. The sketch at the beginning of the last chapter illustrated the All Blacks' pledge to share the leadership baton beyond captain and coach. Author James Kerr identifies shared leadership as one of the hallmarks of the All Blacks' extraordinary success on the playing field.

In this chapter, we explore the concept of flexible deployment as a way of sharing team leadership. A Skills Matrix is a tool for developing a multiskilled team. Multiskilling—using a Skills Matrix—partially dissolves the territorial constraints of job specification, giving jobholders greater oversight and team accountability.

We begin by understanding *specialization* and its pitfalls in the changing world of work. Specialization has, for some time, been a common differentiation strategy. Finding a niche market and dominating it with focused knowledge, products, or services has been a highly effective competitive strategy for over a century. Since the 1980s, marketing gurus have preached the virtues of specialization as a competitive advantage.

Similarly, employees have been fed the same story. To attain job security, develop a specialized skill set, and apply it in a specific field was the mantra. There are numerous illustrations of successful companies adopting a specialization strategy—lending institutions concentrating on home loans and construction companies focusing on commercial property, for example. And there are many examples of employees who've reaped the benefits of specialization. But there's a downside to operating in a niche market or job specialization.

A business striving to corner a market sacrifices its capacity to be maneuverable. An employee too—with a specialist job—has minimal room to move in a rapidly changing job market. Companies specializing in the marketplace replicate this segmentation internally with tightly demarcated boundaries around jobs and functions.

A group of employees clustered together as a team typically have a job specification. For instance, someone is the specialist for administration, another jobholder is the specialist for dealing with the customer or end-user, and another is the technical expert. Even the team leader has a specific job—being the team leader.

This division of labor in the modern workplace is not dissimilar from the Ford Motor Company's assembly line 100 years ago. The organizing of people around specific functions—while doubtlessly efficient—creates challenges for adaptability and responsiveness when needed. Specialization and shared leadership aren't natural bedfellows.

On the surface, erecting clearly defined boundaries around job responsibilities makes sense. Job specification was designed to control work—to make jobholders accountable for a segment of the organization's labor.

However, a smart and agile team, such as the All

Blacks, possesses three attributes. First, it's comprised of highly skilled people. Second, there's a high degree of flexibility within the team's structure. People can move to new positions with relative ease when required to do so. And third, the enterprising team is constantly in a state of honing and refining their skill set. Job specification impedes the last two attributes.

Inherently inflexible job specialization within a team dampens or slows internal mobility. Learning skills outside the explicit limits of the jobholder's job description is discouraged. Can a team embedded in a functional organizational structure achieve the three attributes of agility I just mentioned while reaping the benefits of job specification? I think so.

Before I explain how, consider some other drawbacks of specialization.

First, breaking a job into small, monotonous, and simple component parts makes work dull and repetitive. Boredom leads to absenteeism and other negative consequences. This can lead to disengagement.

Second, specialization puts all the pressure on the leader to manage and be accountable for team output. Team members are left to just do their job. Frederick Taylor's philosophy of *scientific management* paved the way for automating and standardizing work—still virtually universal in today's workplace. On the assembly line—where each worker performs simple tasks in a recurring fashion—the leader is the only person with an objective overview. Shared leadership isn't practical in this organizing structure. Specialization breeds an unhealthy dependency on the leader to manage output. Jobholders don't have a stake in anything other than their immediate work tasks.

Third, creative thinking has no place in a team

segmented into functions. Specialization implies that the specialist *knows best*. Specialists—whether on an assembly line or in the contemporary workplace—are obliged to obediently follow established practices. If a completely new method is considered in a procedure-driven environment, it infers the "old" system is somehow inferior or substandard. This conclusion isn't always easy to accept, especially by the specialist who's well-versed in a conventional procedure—one that may well have been designed by the jobholder. The status quo is understandably vigorously defended. A new method or idea is rejected. The leader is then the sole champion of change.

Fourth, specialization breeds a paint-by-numbers mentality: *this is how we do things, we've always done things this way, and if we follow the system, we'll be successful* are the common catchphrases. These common refrains reinforce the system of specialization.

McDonald's, a modern-day exemplar of specialization, took a long time to change direction and introduce healthy food options into its menu, despite the obvious need. Changing direction is tough going in workplaces consisting of a series of standardized methods and processes, particularly when it has been successful in the past.

A new person with fresh ideas will quickly become frustrated if they are confronted with an endless procession of standardized processes and procedures to follow in their job. In an overly procedurally driven team, questioning the status quo isn't valued to the same extent as maintaining the status quo.

Although job specification is great for holding a jobholder accountable for the work they are supposed to do, it gets in the way when agility is required. Specialization breeds tunnel vision. The jobholder isn't encouraged to understand or appreciate the way the rest of the team and organization operates. Blinkered thinking focuses attention and energy on a few, manageable work tasks—which is the aim of job specialization.

Time for us to turn to a better approach.

Flexible deployment

Flexible deployment—an alternative approach—doesn't abandon job specialization altogether. Flexible deployment entails equipping an employee with a broader range of skills and competencies than mentioned in their original job specification.

The practice of flexible deployment is utilizing the full range of skills and abilities of all team members. The team and its members benefit from flexible deployment as employees maintain their employment relevance by being exposed to and learning a wider range of skills. Flexible work practices are gaining acceptance in the changing workplace, but flexible deployment isn't always introduced systematically, or for the right reasons. When applied in a coordinated fashion, flexibly deploying people's skills builds agility in a team.

Apart from mobilizing agility, a coordinated multiskilling program will encourage team learning—a trait of shared leadership.

Where the rubber meets the road

McDonald's and specialization

One of the biggest success stories of applied scientific management is the McDonald's franchise system.

McDonald's was the first known fast-food restaurant to incorporate the divisions of specialization—one person takes the orders while someone else makes the burgers, another person applies the condiments, and yet another wraps them.

With this level of efficiency, the customer generally receives a product or service with reliable quality. So, if specialization can be applied successfully in McDonald's restaurants, and is now a feature of many fast-food franchise systems, will it continue to be a recipe for success in the future?

Skills Matrix

One of the most effective ways to systemize multiskilling in a team is via a Skills Matrix. This is a simple and practical tool for coordinating a multiskilling program in teams.

Not all team tasks need to be shared and some can be excepted from the Skills Matrix. For example, if a civil engineer is required to sign off on construction work done, this task can't be given to someone else in the team without professional qualifications. However, wherever it's practical to do so, the sharing of tasks ensures that more than one person can perform a team skill to an acceptable standard. The more multiskilled people are, the more agile the team.

Apart from the team's being more agile, employees enhance their employability, as I said earlier. This is a *win–win* situation. Or, if you consider the end-user as well, you might say it's a *win–win–win* situation.

To coordinate and monitor this flexible deployment process, a team must first create its own unique Skills Matrix. A Skills Matrix can be defined as the breakdown and recording of all the tasks in a team that can be shared. Once the tasks have been identified, the next step is to assess the skill level of team members against those tasks. Step three is to coach team members to be proficient in all the tasks in the Skills Matrix.

To inspire a flexible learning culture, team members—if possible—should receive some form of incentive for mastering a range of skills. Mastering skills beyond the scope of their current job description means an individual is more valuable to the team. The adage: *What gets rewarded gets done* is true.

Below in Table 10.1 is an illustration of a Skills Matrix.

Table 10.1 Skills matrix [32]

Team member/Task	1	2	3	4	5	6	7	8	9
Joe									
Mary									
Bill									
Harry									
Sue									
Kathy									

Legend

	Team coach
	Competent
	Undergoing training
	Not yet trained

In the illustration above, six team members are

shown in a skills matrix. Numbers 1 to 9 along the top of the matrix signify nine core tasks needed in that team that can be shared. White spaces in the matrix indicate "Not yet trained." These team members have yet to start their training for that task. Joe requires training in Tasks 6, 7, 8, and 9, for example. He has yet to be exposed to any learning in these areas.

Light grey spaces in the illustrated matrix (Undergoing training) signify that training has commenced for that person in that task. But they have not yet achieved an acceptable standard of performance without close supervision or coaching. For example, Joe has commenced training for Task 1.

Dark grey spaces (Competent) represent tasks where the team member is competent. For example, Joe has achieved mastery in Task 5. Competency is defined as achieving a consistent standard of performance without supervision.

Black spaces (Team coach) identify team coaches. These are people who have achieved a high level of competency in a task and have the job of coaching their fellow team members in that task. For example, Joe is qualified to coach his fellow team members in Tasks 2, 3, and 4. To qualify as a team coach, that individual must have attributes other than a high skill level. They need good communication skills and some basic training in coaching.

As I suggested, a rewards and incentives program can accompany the Skills Matrix, if possible. Using the above illustration, Mary is the most multiskilled of the six within the team—she has achieved competency in five task areas. From a skills perspective, Mary is the most valuable and most crucial member of the team. It would be reasonable for her to be rewarded for learning and applying these team skills. You can also see that Joe, Bill, Kathy, and Mary are team coaches qualified to coach their colleagues in two or more tasks—they're able to share the responsibilities of team development.

The team leader has the overall responsibility for assessing the competency levels across the team. To maintain a consistent standard, the team leader can assess standards and keep the matrix up to date.

The Skills Matrix should be visible for quick reference. Being accessible serves several useful purposes. First, it's a visual representation of the level of multiskilling in the team. The currency of the matrix serves as a reminder to team members to organize themselves to upskill. Second, it's an organizing tool for the leader. For example, in the matrix we refer to, the team leader can ask Sue to find time to commence coaching on Task 1. The leader can also approach Kathy and suggest to her that she should find time to coach Sue throughout the week on that task. And third, the matrix is a visual representation of the extent to which a team is multiskilled. It assists in organizing and motivating the team.

The goal is to have everyone competent in all shared team tasks. Achieving this goal means a team is very agile and more able to withstand sudden shifting priorities imposed on the team from outside.

To be clear, I'm not advocating you completely abandon job descriptions. The Skills Matrix is a useful addition and compensates for skill shortages due to absenteeism or changing circumstances. A multiskilled team can easily share tasks and workloads needed in a rapidly changing and volatile environment.

The Skills Matrix is a simple and powerful multiskilling tool. Team members can be held accountable for learning and deploying their skills in various work situations. The flexible deployment of the team's skill sets is sharing responsibility and leadership.

In the next chapter, we discuss the characteristic of being agile.

The top 10 key points:

1. A Skills Matrix is a tool for developing a multiskilled team.

2. Companies specializing in the marketplace replicate this segmentation internally with tightly demarcated boundaries around jobs and functions.

3. Inherently inflexible job specialization within a team dampens or slows internal mobility.

4. Specialization breeds an unhealthy dependency on the leader to manage output.

5. Although job specification is great for holding a jobholder accountable for the work they are supposed to do, it gets in the way when agility is required.

6. The practice of flexible deployment is utilizing the full range of skills and abilities of all team members in the team's work.

7. One of the most effective ways to systemize multiskilling in a team is via a Skills Matrix.

8. A Skills Matrix can be defined as the breakdown and recording of all the tasks in a team that can be shared.

9. The team leader has the overall responsibility for assessing the competency levels across the team.

10. The Skills Matrix should be visible for quick reference.

CHAPTER 11

Being agile

... the five-year plan is an artefact of the 20ᵗʰ century. The changing team needs a purpose, not a five-year plan.

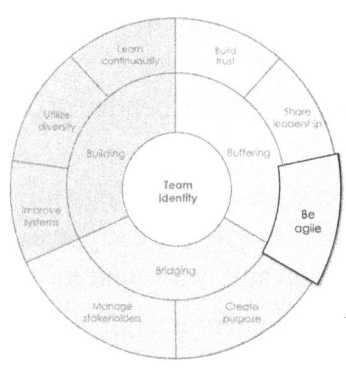

The Australasian Legal Practice Management Association's president, Andrew Barnes, claims that many law firms view technology as a threat instead of a solution. Although 97 percent of the association's members have made some investment in technology, 73 percent believe it's responsible for either a positive or negative change in their firm.

The internet offers a platform for competitors to use non-conventional law firm structures to deliver quality at a lower price. This recent development is putting conventional law firms under pressure to reduce their fees and increase productivity. Technology doubtlessly delivers cost benefits and offers a faster solution.

According to Barnes, automating systems and moving manual tasks online is the answer to delivering services

*at a lower cost with increased responsiveness to the client.
Technology makes it possible for firms to "compete with
people not only in their own town, but across the country,
and some of the providers that are crossing international
borders."*

*Law firms that turn a blind eye to the realities of the
commercial world are playing a dangerous game, warns
Barnes. "The current law firm business model is in danger
of extinction."*[33]

We turn to the third buffering characteristic—being
agile—and its application to performance. Being agile
means adapting rapidly to fluctuations and changes in
the team's external environment. There are seven types of
agility for a team to consider.

Here is an illustration of seven dimensions of agility.

Figure 11.1 Team agility model[34]

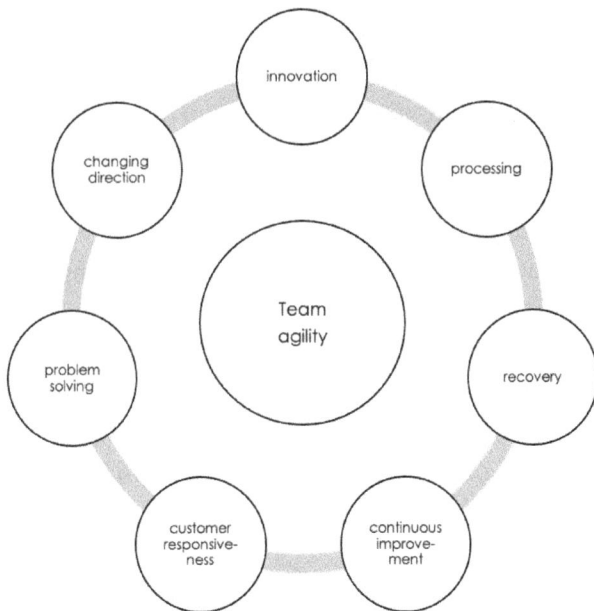

These types of agility shown here are interrelated. Each form feeds off the other six types. Nevertheless, I'll define each type separately. In the next chapter, I will share some tools to promote agility.

I'll start with *innovation*.

Innovation

Innovation means being in the marketplace first with new goods and services that customers want and need. Although many teams don't have direct access to customers, they do have people and units that rely on their work. Innovation involves experimenting with new products and services the customer or the end-user may want. Losing a customer to a pioneering competitor can be the result of a lack of innovation. Or, if an end-user considers a team redundant or behind the times, this ought to be a wake-up call and a reason for innovation.

Product life cycles are getting shorter. First-mover advantage is still a key to business success. Although touch screen technology is now the norm, it wasn't when the iPhone was first released. Being first to market was a colossal advantage to Apple and led to record profits in a short timeframe.

Innovation is, however, more than having bright ideas. We've all thought of a great idea, only to find someone else putting that concept into practice and reaping the rewards. Successful innovation is putting ideas into action rapidly, whether it's a new sought-after product, new services, or an original solution. For this to happen, we need to think and operate differently.

Processing

In terms of a team's agility, *processing* is dispensing everything it does more quickly than its competitors or faster than the end-user's expectation. Speed in processing includes shortening cycle times for managing information, manufacturing products, and delivering services.

For example, the speedy processing of applications for approving finances for an investment property—with the appropriate checks—can give a bank or finance institution an edge over its competitors. Processing speed isn't about cutting corners and forgoing proper QA—it's about getting things done faster without sacrificing quality.

Improving processing speed requires scrutinizing all a team's procedures, systems, and practices. This analysis must also include processes and procedures external to the team. These questions may help:

- Why do we do things this way?
- Is there a better and faster way of administering this transaction?
- What is the purpose of this system?
- Does this process help or hinder outcomes?

Where the rubber meets the road

Automated phone messages

Think about those infuriating automated phone messages we get when we call a company or government department, wanting to speak with a "real" person.

The "voice" typically launches into a long-winded set of instructions, all the while encouraging you to go to the organization's website to complete your transaction. You stubbornly refrain from taking that option because you think it'll be faster to persevere over the telephone. Big mistake!

You subsequently get a nine-option menu to choose from.

By the time you get to option four, you've forgotten what options one, two, and three were. When you get to option nine, you get the option to hear all this again! And then, just as you think your query is about to be answered, the voice tells you that "all operators are busy right now; you have been placed in a queue." The automated voice either instructs you to go through this torture again or tells you that someone (a person, hopefully) will call you back within the next two hours, just as you are about to go into a two-hour meeting.

This is a typical example of poor customer processing speed, all in the interests of "saving" the cost of employing a customer service representative to take your call.[35]

The above illustration is based on the popularly held belief that technology is a most efficient and cost-effective means of communication. But rather than saving costs, this misapprehension does the opposite—it costs money, as customers flee to competitors.

Recovery

Recovery in the context of agility refers to the speed of responding to fixing a mistake. If a customer or end-user feels their complaint is being acknowledged and effectively dealt with in a swift manner, they are often forgiving. Alternatively, if an organization doesn't take responsibility and recover promptly from a mistake, a person is often unforgiving.

A preparedness to fix a mistake assumes that blunders do happen, and when they inevitably do, correcting them without hesitation is the best course of action. A speedy recovery is only possible when someone accepts responsibility and moves to rectify the error.

On the other hand, when a leader doesn't value the actions of a team member to rectify a mistake—and is, instead, fixated on the mistake—it encourages bad behavior. Whatever the mistake—overcharging, sending out the wrong order, or conveying the wrong information—covering it up or pointing the finger of blame elsewhere is the norm when the manager criticizes or punishes the error. It's little wonder, then, that the person at fault doesn't take responsibility for fixing the problem.

These first three types of agility—innovation, processing, and recovery—have one thing in common: speed. Speed is an enabler for agile performance.

Continuous improvement

Continuous improvement is not the same as *innovation*, despite their being often conflated. Innovation is creating something entirely new. Continuous improvement is building upon something that already exists. Well-known inventions such as the motor car, washing machine, and hairdryer are inventions or innovations. Continuous improvement means refining something to make it better. For example, travel luggage with wheels or windscreen wipers on cars.

Business improvements come in many forms. Continuous improvement comes in the following ways:

- *improving* quality
- *increasing* customer responsiveness
- *reducing* costs
- *maximizing* output
- *reducing* safety incidents
- *meeting* deadlines
- *enhancing* cooperation with stakeholders or
- *streamlining* systems and processes.

I'll revisit and elaborate on each of these aspects of continuous improvement in CHAPTER 18 when discussing the characteristic of improving systems.

To be in a constant state of improvement, a team must adopt a whole-of-enterprise approach to performance. This entails being constantly mindful of how functions operate within and outside the team. And the particular place to look for improvement is the link between the component parts that comprise the team system. For instance, when finalizing a report drawing information from several sources, how and when those sources communicate with one another is a useful place to start looking for enhancements.

The other place to look for improvements is within each component part—the functions. For instance, the procedures used, such as how the accountant completes a profit and loss statement. Or the way a salesperson sells a product or service. Team performance is made up of a series of functions and how they interact with one another.

Customer responsiveness

The customer is anybody the team services, whether they're internal or external to the organization. Agility is customer-driven. All seven types of agility affect the customer. Recovery and *customer responsiveness* directly impact the customer. The other five indirectly influence the end-user.

A team cannot afford to ignore or be indifferent to their customers. The customer should be the team's focal point. Ideally, everything in a team that is discussed, thought about, or done should have its customers top of mind.

A team that is customer-responsive responds swiftly and effectively to its end-users. Customer responsiveness is a reactive type of agility unlike, for instance, innovation, which is a proactive behavior. Responsiveness means returning phone calls and responding to email requests promptly, putting a customer or end-user in touch with the right person, and adequately answering questions and helping solve problems. Apart from the right focus, having effective systems and processes in place enhances a team's responsiveness.

Problem-solving

Teams are intricate organisms with an assortment of multi-faceted problems, predicaments, and dilemmas needing attention daily. Workplaces were slower, localized, and predictable in the past. Complex problem-solving is now central to team performance in a multifarious and metamorphic world. The performance systems we use haven't kept pace with change, and they stifle problem-solving capacity.

The rigid, obstinate systemization of our workplaces we discussed in the previous chapter inhibits people from thinking freely. This regimentation began in the early 20th century with the scientific management movement. These systems continue to be used today with franchising and other paint-by-numbers approaches to work. However, in response to a less predictable environment, employees have been told to show initiative, even though they are rewarded for being obedient.

Where the rubber meets the road
Asking for the recipe
I recall staying at a five-star hotel a couple of years ago on a speaking tour throughout South-East Asia. Having just had one of the best meals I've ever eaten in one of the four restaurants in the hotel complex, I decided to approach the receptionist after leaving the restaurant and paying my bill. My wife is a magnificent cook; perhaps I should say, chef! At any rate, I wanted to get a copy of the recipe for this superb Thai dish I'd just had the pleasure of eating to take home for Carol.

The receptionist was positively beaming as I approached her in the hotel's grand foyer. I said to her enthusiastically, "I've just had the most magnificent meal in your Thai restaurant, and I was wondering if you could do me a favor please?" The receptionist, smiling from ear to ear, replied, "Yes, Dr. Baker, I would be happy to help you." "Would it be possible for me to get a copy of the recipe for that meal, please?" I blurted out, with a copy of the menu clutched in my hand.

The receptionist's demeanor changed instantly and dramatically. Mild panic swept across her face—she went as white as a ghost! The smile vanished into thin air. The receptionist was undoubtedly thinking to herself at this point—*what am I going to do?* I could see that she wanted to dive under the reception desk and look for the procedures manual to tell her what to do in this unusual situation.

Of course, this kind of request wouldn't be documented anywhere. She had to think on her feet, literally. This is an example of a challenging problem that team members face regularly—mostly with frontline teams dealing with the demanding public—where there is no obvious solution. After much consultation with the reception team leader, I received the recipe!

Many roadblocks prevent team members from displaying suitable initiative to solve these kinds of predicaments—ones they encounter more and more. Team members aren't generally taught to problem-solve, which is surprising, considering the greater frequency of one-off dilemmas they face in the changing world. So, when confronted by a unique situation that needs resolving, employees tend to default to a stock-standard answer in the procedures manual, assuming, of course, there is an answer! They understandably play it safe. *Sorry sir (or madam), I can't help you. It's not within our scope* is the archetypal inflexible response we've all been accustomed to. Problem-solving agility is conveniently bypassed, despite its relevance to performance.

Changing direction

The agility to change direction is the zenith of the other six dimensions in the Team Agility model. To illustrate:

- *innovating* is changing direction
- *processing* faster is changing normal practice
- *recovering* from a mistake means changing course
- *continuous improvement* is changing something through enhancement
- *customer responsiveness* is shifting priorities to cater to the need of a customer and
- *problem-solving* is often about changing the way one thinks about a situation.

So, agility is ultimately about changing direction.

A team needs many types of agility to change direction. Changing circumstances may involve the emergence of a new market, such as building a housing estate to accommodate an influx of miners to an area next to a new mine site. Or a change of government and new priorities and laws, such as reductions in immigration intakes. Or changes in economic conditions, such as a sudden downturn in economic activity, which can have a severe and sudden impact on revenue in the tourist or entertainment industries. To accommodate these external vicissitudes, a team needs to change in several ways to be responsive.

Teams need to react to inevitable ups and downs, new priorities, and shifting markets. Without responding by changing direction, a team faces two problems. First, the team misses beneficial opportunities that pass by. A team lacking the agility to change direction can't take advantage of an opening. Second, the relevance and viability of a team are threatened if it is entrenched in its ways. Consider Kodak, the local independent hamburger shop, and the local butcher. All perished or face the threat of extinction because they were, or are, too slow to respond to the changing needs of the marketplace.

Being flexible and maneuverable is difficult, however; there are myriad barriers and obstacles. One stumbling block is the outdated notion that it's the leader's job to establish certainty and clarity. How can a leader be sure about their direction in an ambiguous and ever-changing landscape? What's more, when confronted with a sudden, necessary, and unexpected course correction, the leader embracing this archaic idea will hesitate.

The idea that leaders are supposed to offer certainty and clarity is deeply engrained. Traditional leaders, for instance, strive to build and follow a comprehensive strategic plan. But the five-year plan is an artefact of the 20th century. The changing team needs a purpose, not a *five-year plan* (see CHAPTER 13).

With the five-year plan in place, front and center, an unanticipated and abrupt change in direction implies the leader has miscalculated, or not forecasted, future events and circumstances. Subsequently, the leader loses face with a direction about-face. So, not wanting to appear incompetent—and with certainty and clarity—the conventional leader chooses to stay the original course. And a great opportunity may go begging.

In the next chapter, we consider four non-job roles essential for agile performance.

The top 10 key points

1. Being agile means adapting rapidly to fluctuations and changes in the team's external environment. There are seven types of agility for a team to consider.

2. The seven types of agility are interrelated.

3. Innovation means being in the marketplace first with new goods and services that customers want and need.

4. In terms of a team's agility, processing is dispensing everything it does more quickly than its competitors or faster than the end-user's expectation.

5. Recovery in the context of agility refers to the speed of responding to fixing a mistake.

6. Continuous improvement is building upon something that already exists.

7. A team that is customer responsive responds swiftly and effectively to its end-users.

8. Complex problem-solving is now central to team performance in a multifarious and metamorphic world.

9. The agility to change direction is the zenith of the other six dimensions in the Team Agility model.

10. Agility is ultimately about changing direction.

CHAPTER 12

Elevating non-job roles essential for agile performance

Questioning the status quo is the new black. Being prepared to challenge the way things are done is the hallmark of a successful team.

Fluorescent elastic bands and grown men in giant jolly jumpers. You could be excused for thinking the All Blacks have gone all New Age in their quest for success.

Not according to the team's long-time strength and conditioning coach, Nic Gill, who says the multi-colored bands have become vital tools in attaining a physical edge.

And, while some of the training field activities might look a bit whacky, Gill says that rather than dreaming up new methods, he focused on keeping things as simple as possible.

"When I was younger, I fell into that trap, but really it's about doing the basic things that have got them where they are as a player and helping them do them better."[36]

In the prior chapter, we covered seven types of team agility. Job specification is a roadblock to agile performance. By shifting from a job focus to a performance focus, a team has the right environment in which to display initiative in the right circumstances. Teams need to break free of the job specification stranglehold that asphyxiates agile performance.

Here we consider four non-job roles and how they promote agility.

The work people do in a team is two-dimensional; there are job tasks and non-job tasks.

Although non-job tasks are critical for team success, the job description emphasizes job tasks and understates non-job tasks. Leaders need to elevate non-job tasks.

The transformative changes of the late 20th century shone a spotlight on work performance and the systems we use to support it. Job description formats have stayed reasonably constant since the 1950s. While some evolution has occurred, the job description still focuses primarily on the job role.

The job description captures the job dimension of performance, but agility comes from non-job behavior. A performance focus that fosters agile behavior eventuates from at least four non-job roles. Elevating the status of these non-job roles is the first step in encouraging agile team performance.

Non-job performance

Non-job performance isn't job-specific. Furthermore, exercising non-job roles is as relevant to team performance as the proper execution of job tasks. It's now widely acknowledged that having a positive and enthusiastic attitude, displaying teamwork, developing one's self, and contributing to improving the way the team functions are vital for performance. Yet these behaviors are non-job-specific and therefore rarely, if ever, stated in the job description.

But it's clear that employees who are enterprising and enthusiastic team players, willing to grow and develop their capabilities and suggest ways to improve team efficiencies and effectiveness, are an asset. Although not documented in the job description, these attributes are contributors to team performance.

By placing more attention on these non-job behaviors, leaders are enabling many of the types of agility we discussed in the previous chapter. For instance, team performance can be boosted by morale-lifting behavior such as being positive and enthusiastic under adversity, sacrificing self-interest for the sake of the team, learning and applying a new skill on the job, and coming up with a new and better way of doing something that benefits the team. These non-job behaviors improve recovery, customer-responsiveness, and continuous improvement, to name a few types of agility.

Everyone profits from applying these non-job roles. A team member—when exercising the full extent of their non-job roles—adds value to their current job role and improves their employability. For the ambitious employee, notable team contributions outside the scope of their job description, such as the non-job roles mentioned, are likely to enhance their career prospects. A team leader gains from fully engaging the hearts and minds of team members. And the customer or end-user benefits from speedier response rates, innovative services and products, and better solutions.

In the past, employees were only praised for their reliability and conscientiousness in fulfilling the literal requirements of their job specification. Sticking stringently to the letter of their job description was, and in most cases still is, expected. Progressive leaders, however, expect their people to be enterprising—to behave beyond the scope of their job description.

Figure 12.1 below illustrates a more expansive framework of work performance that considers four non-job roles.

Figure 12.1 Model of work performance[37]

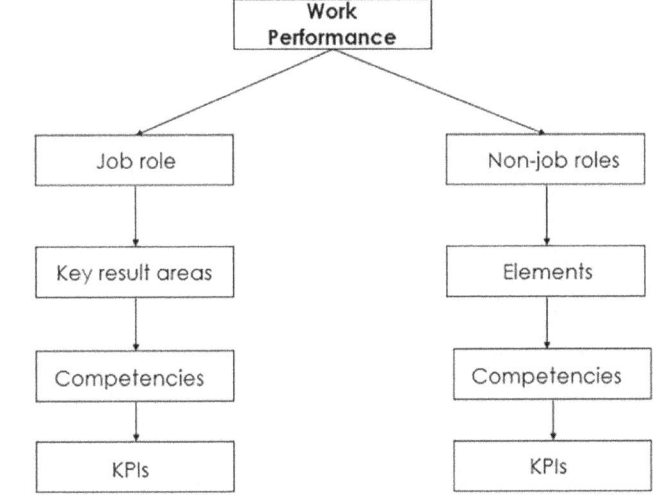

The standard job description covers the *Job role, Key result areas, Competencies,* and *KPIs,* shown on the left-hand side of Figure 12.1. The non-job dimension of performance consists of Non-job roles, Elements, Competencies, and KPIs, displayed on the right. In effect, this means that total performance consists of five roles—one job role and four non-job roles.

Before I describe these four non-job roles in more detail, let me reinforce the importance and relevance of non-job behavior to agile performance. What do you think are the attributes that employers value most in employees? The top 10 most-valued job skills have been compiled from over 40 studies of medium- and large-scale employers, primarily in the United States but also in other countries such as Australia, France, Singapore, and the UK.

These top 10 job skills are:

1. Enthusiasm/positive attitude

2. Good communication skills

3. Self-motivation/initiative

4. Honesty

5. A liking for people

6. Persistence

7. Ability to work in a team

8. Good organizational skills/ability to work well under pressure

9. Willingness to learn

10. Dependability/good work ethic[38]

All 10 of these attributes are valuable in any team, in professional, semi-professional, and non-professional vocations, blue-collar or white-collar industries, and indoor or outdoor work environments. They have universal appeal.

When recruiting potential employees, these are the attributes contemporary employers look for, apart from technical qualifications and experience. Once an employee is selected and commences employment, however, these non-job attributes aren't formally recognized as part of the performance framework.

The number of potential roles an employee can perform at work is limitless. Some are consciously performed, others instinctively carried out. Some are relevant, some not. Some take a split second to execute, others are ongoing. Some are appreciated, some not. Some are rewarded, most aren't. So, what are the universally applicable non-job roles team members can perform that support agile performance?

Where the rubber meets the road

A definition of agility in the world of sport

Agility is the complex skill of rapid multidirectional movement incorporating variations to velocity and the manipulation of momentum. Agility skill execution is a feature of open-skilled sports such as rugby union and represents a fundamental component of successful performance.[39]

The non-job role framework

There are four non-job roles I have identified that are increasingly important in any team's performance. Together these four roles constitute the non-job role framework. These include:

- a positive attitude and enthusiasm role
- a team role
- a skill development role and
- an innovator and continuous improvement role.[40]

Referring to the top 10 job skills I outlined above, there are many other roles—apart from the four listed—that employers consider significant. Nonetheless, I will justify the relevance of the four non-job roles in the framework for agile team performance. Off the bat, these four are applicable across all industries and directly or indirectly associated with agility.

Two of the roles in the framework are interpersonal attributes and the other two are personal attributes.

Interpersonal non-job roles

Let's start with the *positive attitude and enthusiasm* role. It's a big bonus to oneself and everyone else one interacts with at work to be positive and enthusiastic (or anywhere else, for that matter). Being negative and lacking enthusiasm *all* the time is impossible. Although I've worked with some people that test this claim! People's attitudes undoubtedly affect those around them. That is why I have classified the positive attitude and enthusiasm role as interpersonal, despite one's attitude being a personal choice.

It's not an unreasonable expectation for people to maintain—most of the time—a positive attitude and enthusiasm at work. Enthusiasm and a positive attitude are # 1 on the list of job skills mentioned earlier. With considerable pressure on a team to be in a constant and rapid state of chop and change, being positive is necessary for building and preserving high morale. This role helps a team cope with relentless adjustments and disruptions.

Upholding a positive attitude and being enthusiastic is an antidote to modern-day pressures and stresses. Cultivating a harmonious working environment is undeniably important for a team. It's hardly unsurprising, therefore—with the strains of contemporary life—that it's first on the list of most-wanted attributes at work.

Next is the *team* role. With the flattening of organizational structures, teams are rapidly becoming the main organizing work structure. Being a team player is a sought-after quality. Employees now are expected to participate in short- and long-term project teams, often with people they have never met, let alone worked with before. These project teams are designed to solve specific cross-functional problems and challenges, drawing upon employees with a broad spectrum of expertise and perspectives.

Ability to work in a team (team role) is seventh on the list of the most-valued job skills. Playing the team role is a multifaceted combination of attitude and interpersonal skills. Working successfully in a team means having, for instance,

- the capacity to influence and be open to being influenced by others
- the ability to juggle the dual responsibilities of individual and team outputs
- the aptitude to work cooperatively and harmoniously with others, often under duress, and
- the willingness and ability to interact and exchange information with a variety of stakeholders.

This non-job role is becoming even more germane to organizational performance.

Personal non-job roles

The first of the two personal non-job roles in the

framework is the skill development role. This role involves continually growing and developing technically and personally. Being a lifelong learner is more than a cliché—it's critical to success. Despite this, we know people who've stopped learning and developing—*I'm too old to learn anything new* is a familiar refrain. Or, when invited to learn something new to potentially benefit themselves and their career, some people say, *I'm just happy doing what I have always done.* But there's no doubting that improving, upgrading, and expanding a person's capabilities benefits them, their career, and the team.

The ninth most-valuable job skill is a *willingness to learn.* Having a readiness to learn means being open to different perspectives and ways of doing things and receptive to feedback.

There are two aspects that make up the skill development role. One relates to technical development. This part is concerned with education, training, and career decisions. The second aspect involves self-development. Personal development covers a host of things, including managing time and priorities, people skills, and minimizing stress.

Although listed as a personal role in the framework, individual skill development benefits others too. Being open-minded to new possibilities and opportunities and contemplating problems and challenges in more sophisticated ways benefit others in the team.

The final role in the framework is *innovation and continuous improvement.* While the skill development role betters the individual, the innovation and continuous improvement role improves the work setting.

A person practicing innovation and continuous improvement offers constructive suggestions regarding how the team functions. This non-job role covers a wide range of goals. It can include:

- increasing team output
- reducing time and costs for getting things done
- increasing safety and well-being
- meeting deadlines, enhancing interpersonal cooperation or
- streamlining systems and processes.

These factors were briefly mentioned in the last chapter. For a team surrounded by a world of warp speed and ambiguity, to prosper it needs to be in a constant state of growth and renewal. All team members should be responsible for innovation and continuous improvement. Number three on the top 10 list, *self-motivation/initiative*, is aligned with team regeneration.

More specifically, taking responsibility for originating tasks, new ideas, and methods, and the ability to think and act without being prompted, are apropos for agile performance. Getting everyone engaged in furthering the efficiency and effectiveness of the team, however, has been a perennial challenge since Peter Senge coined the term *learning organization* over a quarter of a century ago.

Enriching the work setting is still predominantly considered the province of the leader, not their team members. But the responsibility for bettering the working environment should fall on the shoulders of all members of the team—not just on the shoulders of the leader.

Gaining a competitive advantage is the ultimate driver of business success. And acquiring the edge and retaining relevance come from being adaptable and maneuverable. *Doing things like we always have* isn't going to cut it anymore. Questioning the status quo is the new black. Being prepared to challenge the way things are done is the hallmark of a successful team.

Each of the four non-job roles stimulates agility in its own way. Non-job roles are unappreciated—despite our recognizing them as important—in traditional work-based performance systems. Specialization and an over-reliance on the job description are the primary stumbling block to agile behavior.

So, how can you better utilize these non-job roles?

Discuss these four non-job roles with your team and embed them in the work document we call a job description. Ask these questions for each non-job role:

- *What* does this role mean?
- *Why* is it important in our team?
- *What* are some key elements of this role?
- *How* can we determine if we are exercising this role?

Once you reach common ground, add the four non-job roles to everyone's job specification, with some KPIs. Contextualize them to your team setting. Refer to them frequently.

To fully appreciate the benefit of these non-job roles, consider the effect of a team practicing the opposite. Imagine everyone in your team displaying a consistently negative attitude, acting as individuals without regard for the team, no longer growing and developing, and leaving the responsibility for team improvement solely to you as leader. A scary thought!

Get to work.

The roles of having a positive attitude and enthusiasm, being a team player, developing oneself technically and personally, and contributing to business improvement are widely regarded as vital employee attributes. These four non-job roles are in high demand across all industries, as the research suggests. Promoting these attributes breaks the stranglehold of job specification and encourages agile team behavior.

So far in PART II, we've considered three characteristics of high-performing teams: building trust, sharing leadership, and being agile. Each of these characteristics assists a team to protect itself from the relentless pressure of outside influences that can destroy the team's cohesion.

In CHAPTER 13, we move from buffering to bridging. The first of two characteristics to externally build bridges with stakeholders is *creating purpose*.

The top 10 key points

1. The work people do in a team is two-dimensional; there are job tasks and non-job tasks.

2. Leaders need to elevate non-job tasks.

3. It's a big bonus to oneself and everyone else one interacts with at work to be positive and enthusiastic (or anywhere else for that matter).

4. Upholding a positive attitude and being enthusiastic can be an antidote to modern-day pressures and stresses.

5. With the flattening of organizational structures, teams are rapidly becoming the main organizing

work structure. Being a team player is a sought-after quality.

6. Playing the team role is a multifaceted combination of attitude and interpersonal skills.

7. The first of the two personal non-job roles in the framework is the skills development role.

8. The skills development role involves continually growing and developing technically and personally.

9. The final role in the framework is innovation and continuous improvement.

10. A person practicing innovation and continuous improvement offers constructive suggestions regarding how the team functions.

CHAPTER 13

Creating purpose

If people don't know where they're headed, anywhere is good enough.

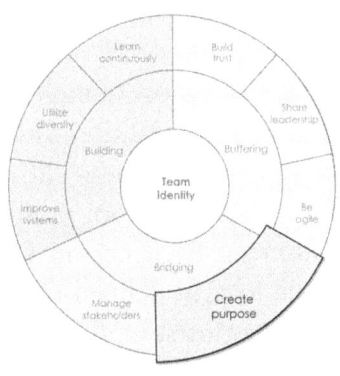

Soon after a long, painful flight back from South Africa landed, eight men found a small meeting room in the headquarters of the New Zealand Rugby Union and sat down to "fix this thing."

In the room were coach Graham Henry, his assistants Smith and Hansen, Enoka, the mental skills coach, the team manager, Brian Lochore, All Blacks captain Tana Umaga, and his then vice-captain, Richie McCaw. The meeting lasted three days.

Graham Henry describes it as the most important conversation of his All Blacks career. It would result in the complete overhaul of the most successful sporting culture in human history.

The key insight came from the old warhorse, Brian Lochore. Pondering the strategic objective—to create "an environment ... that would stimulate the players and make

them want to take part in it"—he came up with six words
that would define the efforts of the next eight or so years:
—Better People Make Better All Blacks.[41]

In this chapter, I consider seven issues that can derail a team's purpose. Creating purpose is the first of two characteristics in the Team Identity model that support the bridging function of team identity. In the next chapter, I'll share a useful team exercise to develop a team purpose statement.

Purpose in the world of sport is a simple proposition. It's essentially about winning—winning the set, winning the half, winning the game, winning the tournament. Winning is the name of the game in sport.

In the world of business, purpose is more complex. There are myriad moving parts in organizations, and everyone is a small cog in the wheel of production. Ultimately, winning is the purpose of business, too: more sales, more revenue, more customers. Each person in an organization has a specific role to play, defined by a job description. But unlike sport, there are several scoreboards, mostly out of sight and often out of mind.

Graham Kenny, in his Harvard Business Review article *Your Corporate Purpose Will Ring Hollow If the Company's Actions Don't Back It Up*, states:

> Purpose looks at the organization from the outside to consider the difference that a business makes in people's lives.[42]

Creating purpose is based on how others outside the team benefit. This differs from the sport's world, too. Winning a game will surely satisfy a sporting team's supporters. But the sports team focuses entirely on itself and its execution. If a team plays better than its opposition, it wins, and its supporters are happy. Purpose in business is giving the end-user what they want. The focus is external to the team, and the purpose can vary, depending on the needs of the end-user.

What is the value a team generates for its customers and stakeholders? is the key question for the business team. After understanding the needs of its end-users, a team can begin formulating its purpose. Operational activity within a team is obviously important, but only to the extent that it meets the requirements of the team's end-users. The team's relationship with its stakeholders is therefore critical to success.

Employees aren't always clear about their purpose, however. Using the forest analogy: jobholders can't see the forest for the trees. Day by day, they have their heads pressed up against a large tree and can't see the surrounding forest. So the leader's job is to pull the jobholder back from the tree every now and then, long enough for them to see the forest.

Preferably, everything that is thought about, said, and done in a team environment (operational activity) is on purpose, either directly or indirectly. All decisions are made through the prism of team purpose. Resolving problems, overcoming challenges, and facing dilemmas should be purpose-driven. Roles and responsibilities should be shaped around team purpose. Conflicts are resolved with purpose in mind. Expenditure decisions should be evaluated against purpose. Priorities are to be in sync with purpose. Learning and development experiences are sought out and designed to build greater capacity to better meet purpose. This is what should happen, but it's not always what happens, as we know.

Operational activity starts with a clear purpose and direction. If people don't know where they're headed, anywhere is good enough.

Where the rubber meets the road

Three famous purpose statements

To refresh the world in body, mind and spirit. (Coca-Cola)

Apple is committed to bringing the best personal computing experience to students, educators, creative professionals and consumers around the world through its innovative hardware, software and Internet offerings. (Apple)

Our aim is to make the best possible ice cream, in the nicest possible way. (Ben & Jerry)

Notice these purpose statements have three common traits:

Their value proposition – What's the value they are adding?

Their target market – Who are the people they are targeting?

Their channels/methods – How do they intend to go about achieving that value proposition to the target market?[43]

We all face innumerable distractions every day. Some are significant, most, less so. Distraction is always relentless and sometimes seductive. Other teams we work with can have different agendas and priorities, and these can change without notice, and in a blink of an eye.

Busyness is virtuous. If someone's busy—with their head down and tail up—they often avoid getting into strife. Busyness can take priority over attention to purpose.

What's more, we're addicted to the urgent over the important. If deadlines are being met, we claim to be efficient. But the real questions are: *Am I effective? Am I doing the right thing, at the right time, with the right people, in the right way?* Being clear and committed to purpose is the precursor of effectiveness.

Knowing the purpose is only the starting point. Buying into purpose is even better. Purpose in action is complicated for the individual and the team.

As team leader, you should consider these seven questions:

1. Do I know my team's purpose?

2. Have I communicated this purpose to all team members?

3. Do my team members understand its purpose and their role?

4. Do all team members accept the purpose?

5. Are all team members committed to the purpose?

6. Do all team members know how their work is tracking against the team's purpose?

7. Am I supporting my team to achieve the team purpose?

I'll briefly elaborate on each question—they go to the heart of creating and maintaining purpose.

Knowing purpose

If I asked you to define in one sentence what the core purpose of your team is, would you be able to confidently blurt out something coherent? Or would you balk? Would you be happy with your response? Would you be eager to change it or add something to your initial response? The bottom line: If you are having trouble articulating your team's purpose, you can be confident your team members will struggle too.

Communicating purpose

If you're clear about your team's purpose, have you communicated this purpose to your team? Not once or twice, but daily. Communicating purpose is never-ending—it should be done consistently and persistently. It's always the same message (purpose), and every opportunity is taken to share it.

What would happen if I randomly asked one of your team members if you'd communicated the team's purpose to them? Would they say yes? Could they remember the last time you did this?

Communicating purpose can be done verbally or in writing. Are all tasks, projects, and activities your team does aligned with team purpose?

Most daily interruptions at work aren't purpose-related but probably need doing, nonetheless. Then there's work that's not obviously connected to purpose but may eventually contribute to achieving purpose. It's a minefield, and that's why communicating purpose relentlessly is so important.

Understanding purpose

Communicating purpose doesn't mean it's understood. *Do team members comprehend the team's purpose? Are team members aware of how their work contributes to team purpose? Is purpose expressed simply, or is it too cumbersome to grasp?* Purpose is the driver for all team action, energy, and thought.

Merely asking if someone understands the purpose can be misleading. Most will say *yes, I understand it*, even if they don't. It's the priorities and actions of team members that ultimately determine whether purpose is comprehended.

Accepting purpose

It's one thing to understand the purpose, it's another to accept it. People walk past the purpose plaque on the wall daily—they may even be able to recite the words and understand its meaning. But they can also dismiss it as "just words" with little or no relevance to their real work. Team members often consider the purpose statement as an academic exercise, with no practical relevance to their day-to-day work.

The challenge is to embrace the purpose—to accept it—and apply it day by day, moment by moment, situation by situation.

Purpose is concerned with *why* we do what we do, not *how* we do our work. Further, the why of work should be focused on the beneficiaries of that work. *What value do I provide the end-user?* is the question someone who understands and accepts their purpose can answer.

Your team might be an internal service provider. Or it might service the needs of customers external to the business. Either way, *how can we make the lives of the people the team serves better?* is the question to ponder. Answering this question is at the heart of a team's purpose and guides its everyday decisions and actions.

Committing to purpose

Accepting purpose goes some way to being committed to it. But acceptance and commitment are different concepts. Accept the purpose doesn't necessarily mean being committing to it.

Being truly committed to something means having an emotional attachment to it. Commitment to purpose goes beyond understanding and acceptance.

Emotional commitment is demonstrated in many ways. People who are committed to a purpose come to work fired up, full of energy, and clear on what needs to be done that day—they go the extra mile. No shortcuts. No sloppiness. Contagious camaraderie—a willingness to cooperate and cut through. Gaining emotional buy-in to a purpose is the holy grail and a hallmark of all successful teams.

Sustaining that commitment over time is challenging and rare. Some might say, any commitment is rare! But even the most committed teams lose oxygen from time to time. Circumstances changes. Barriers are erected. Mistakes made. Support withdrawn. Discouragement, distraction, setbacks, misunderstandings, and failures test resolve and commitment. Commitment needs refueling like a car needs petrol, diesel, or electricity.

Getting commitment to purpose is easier in some industries. In the not-for-profit sector, for instance, it's relatively easier to get commitment from those working for a cause, such as serving the homeless.

For example, Felicity works for a charity that supports homeless youth. She is drawn to that cause. This challenge has greater emotional resonance for Felicity than issuing invoices and completing mundane administrative tasks in a government office. But that doesn't mean her commitment to homeless youth won't be tested occasionally.

Even working in these kinds of work environments—with their natural advantages—commitment can't be taken for granted. Leaders need to prime the pump daily. Communicating a clear line of sight between the work people do and the value it creates is even more relevant when there's no obvious emotional attachment to the work.

Feedback on the purpose

Feedback is vital—it's important in all walks of life. Humans need feedback. That's why our society has an abundance of regulations, rules, and legislation. We want to know where the line in the sand is. Knowing where we stand doesn't mean we won't overstep the line from time to time. We will. Frequently. Nonetheless, people need feedback for their psychological safety.

What's more, when it's pointed out that we've overstepped the mark, we don't necessarily react well to the feedback. But people want to know the *rules*. Guidelines play to our fundamental human need for security.

When receiving feedback, we can be affronted and defensive. Feedback reminds us that we are off track and need to make a course correction. Despite possible resistance, the resistor to the feedback still needs to hear the feedback. Just because we don't like hearing it doesn't mean we don't need the feedback.

Purpose and feedback go together. *How are people tracking against the team's core purpose? When and how have they gone off track? How can they get back on track?* are questions the leader needs to communicate with team members regularly.

Supporting purpose

Many obstacles pave the road to achieving purpose. Some roadblocks are obvious and others less so. Attending mindless meetings—with no relevance to the core business of the team—is a palpable barrier, for instance. Vested interests and organizational politics that interfere with a team's purpose are less tangible, but obstructive. Barriers come in many forms.

There are major and minor roadblocks. Some obstacles are unavoidable and need to be dealt with resourcefully; others are avoidable. Stumbling blocks can be time pressures, bureaucratic distractions, differing agendas, a lack of clarity, budget constraints, and many others. Removing these roadblocks partially or fully, wherever possible, is the leader's job.

Anticipating roadblocks and paving a way forward is necessary to stay on purpose. When obstacles arrive out of the blue, the team leader's job is to remove them or work around them. Regardless of what they are or where they come from, they are the enemy of staying on purpose.

Whichever way these hurdles arrive, they deplete energy and divert it away from purpose. Without minimizing the impact or eliminating barriers altogether, morale and productivity take an inevitable nosedive. Roadblocks test team resolve.

These seven questions are crucial for staying on purpose and managing expectations. They offer you a framework for creating and sustaining team purpose.

In the next chapter, I will provide you with a useful exercise to formulate your team purpose.

The top 10 key points

1. Creating purpose is based on how others outside the team benefit.

2. Everything that is thought about, said, and done in a team environment is on purpose, either directly or indirectly.

3. There are seven questions a team leader must ask to create and sustain purpose.

4. Do I know the team's purpose?

5. Have you communicated this purpose to all team members?

6. Do your team members understand its purpose and their role?

7. Do all team members accept the purpose?

8. Are all team members committed to the purpose?

9. Do all team members know how their work is tracking against the team's purpose?

10. Are you supporting your team to achieve the team purpose?

CHAPTER 14
Developing team purpose

A well-crafted purpose statement defines the team's raison d'être—why it exists, why it was formed, why it's needed, and how it adds value.

Now that we've covered the relevance of purpose in the previous chapter, we'll consider a collaborative team exercise to develop a team purpose statement. Creating purpose—the first of three characteristics supporting the bridging function of team identity—helps to galvanize the team and focus its attention on servicing its stakeholders and customers.

The purposeless team

A team without a clear and compelling purpose gets side-tracked easily and frequently. The purposeless team is busy working on activity that isn't always useful and neglects tasks pivotal to its purpose. This misalignment between what's done and what should be done leads to frustration, poor morale, and low performance. The aimless team also rapidly establishes a reputation for ineffectiveness by those it interacts with and relies upon.

A team without purpose substitutes busyness for achievement. Team members—unsure of their role, although active—lack vision and clarity. Meanwhile, stakeholders and customers—often having a better understanding of the team's core purpose—become frustrated and disillusioned. Relationships fray. People fall short of expectations. Mediocre performance prevails.

Without purpose, a team can't assess its performance. Lacking constant and purpose-driven behavior, the purposeless team is oblivious to its poor performance, although the sub-standard performance is apparent to the end-users, who depend on the aimless team to deliver results.

A well-crafted purpose statement defines the team's raison d'être—why it exists, why it was formed, why it's needed, and how it adds value. *How should we behave to achieve our purpose? What are the values, norms, and behaviors that are consistent with our purpose?* are the questions that are easier to answer with a purpose statement.

This exercise I'm about to share remedies the undesirable consequences of a purposeless team.

Team purpose and behavior agreement

This exercise has been adapted from an exercise by *Hyper Island*.[44] It's been modified, based on my experience of implementing purpose statements with numerous teams over many years.

The activity has two parts and is designed to facilitate a team purpose and identity a set of guiding behaviors. It's simple, collaborative, and takes very little time to accomplish. It's very effective, however. It clarifies why the team exists and identifies the behaviors necessary to promote its purpose. Two questions are addressed in this activity: *Why do we exist? And how should we behave?* Defining a purpose and an associated set of behaviors helps the team focus on its important work.

The team leader facilitates a dialog on the best way the team can work together. The goal in this conversation is to create a visual manifestation of the team's purpose and the proper actions that fulfill that purpose.

Where the rubber meets the road

A purpose is like a coat hanger

A purpose statement is like a coat hanger in a closet. We all have too many coat hangers, right? They seem to breed!

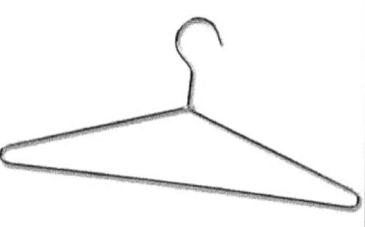

Coat hangers are useless on their own—they can even be downright annoying. No one pays too much attention to the humble coat hanger, and they take up too much space amongst our clothes.

However, the coat hanger has a purpose—it's very useful for hanging garments off. What's more, the coat hanger helps to shape the item of clothing hanging from it.

This is also the reason for a team purpose statement. Ideally, everything that's said, done, and thought about in a team should be consistent with its core purpose.

The way we approach work; the way we treat each other and our important stakeholders and customers; the way we problem-solve; the way we reward each other; the way we measure our success, and so on, should reflect the team's purpose statement.

A purpose statement is an indispensable and under-rated tool that guides and informs every decision made in the team. [45]

The first part of the structured conversation is to form a vibrant purpose statement. The second part of the team discussion is to develop a set of relevant behaviors consistent with that purpose. The two parts go together but may be two separate conversations.

Ask the team to reflect on these questions to begin with:

- *What* is our role as a team?
- *What* is our main goal?
- *How* should we define success?
- *What* benefits do we bring to our end-users or customers?

I'd suggest asking team members to consider these questions before meeting together. Coming to the meeting prepared enriches the conversation. These are questions you want everyone to think about. So, give team members time to contemplate these questions. To facilitate this occurring, send a reminder several days before the designated team meeting.

For this to be an effective exercise, you need everyone to be involved—it's not optional to opt out of this exercise. Some may initially see this as a frivolous activity and a waste of time. That's understandable. Persevere. Just hold the line and be patient.

At the team meeting, invite each person to share their thoughts and ideas based on these questions. Record this information.

After everyone has shared their responses, you've set the scene to create a team purpose statement. Asking these four questions and giving people adequate time to reflect works better than spontaneously asking: *What's our purpose?*

Time now to consider the ingredients of a good purpose statement.

Adding to the three purpose statements in the previous chapter, here are some more purpose statements from well-known companies:

> *Build the best product, cause no unnecessary harm, use business to inspire and implement solutions to the environmental crisis.* (Patagonia)

> *The Earth's most customer-centric company, where customers can find and discover anything they might want to buy online.* (Amazon)

> *To ensure the ability of the earth to nurture life in all its diversity.* (Greenpeace)

> *To give people the power to share and make the world more open and connected.* (Facebook)

To organize the world's information and make it universally accessible and useful. (Google)

Share these examples—they illustrate what a constructive purpose statement looks like.

In brief, a good purpose statement is

- inspirational
- expressed in a single sentence
- focused on one key driver
- concentrated on the end-user and
- created collaboratively.

Let's look at each element briefly.

Inspirational

The statement should inspire—it ought to motivate and uplift.

We provide good services to our internal customers

is lackluster and unlikely to rouse team members to higher performance.

Short

A good purpose statement is brief as well as inspirational. Purpose statements that are a paragraph or page long aren't read, let alone internalized by those they are for, or anyone else, for that matter. One sentence is enough. One sentence forces you to get to the point. Capturing the crux of what your team aspires to in a few words is best.

Key driver

Inspiring and brief, a purpose should focus on one key driver. In the examples I shared above, you'll notice words and phrases such as "best product"; "customer-centric"; "the power to share"; and "universally accessible." The one key driver condenses all the blood, sweat, and tears of team activity down to one focal point.

End-user

The statement, aside from being inspirational, brief, and concentrated on one focal point, should emphasize the end-user. It states whom the team services. Is it a select group of external customers or stakeholders? Is the team serving an internal customer? Or both? By identifying the "customer," the team is mindful of its decisions and their impact on the end-user. Questions to consider:

- What are the needs of the customer?
- How best can we fulfill those needs? (Is it speed? Is it precision? Is it value for money? Is it timeliness? Is it quality?)

Collaborative

And finally, the purpose statement is formed collaboratively. Everyone in the team has an input.

If it's constructed by the leader, they will undoubtedly be sold on the statement. But ... probably no one else will be as excited and enthusiastic about it, no matter how great it is. To be relevant and enabling, the purpose statement must be *owned* by the team. Therefore, everyone must have a stake in its development—it's a team effort.

After everyone has shared their responses to the

four questions posed earlier, ask each person to write their version of the team's purpose, mindful of the five elements I've just covered. Invite them to consider their purpose individually first. Otherwise, some may sit back passively and let others control the process. The objective is to attain complete ownership of whatever statement emerges.

To illustrate, if there are six members of the team, including the team leader, six statements are formed initially.

It may appear nightmarish to merge several individual statements into one overall statement. This may seem even more demanding when there is a diversity of viewpoints. Relax. Remember this: it will be more chaotic and time-consuming trying to create one statement from scratch. Stay with me.

I've found that the following approach works wonders for arriving at a single purpose statement that everyone has a stake in.

Once each team member has crafted their version of the purpose statement, they then pair up. Each person shares their statement with their partner. Together, they formulate a statement that incorporates the best of both individual purpose statements. The aim here is to end up with one statement that both people are satisfied with.

Let me illustrate what I mean. Here is an example of one statement:

> To provide quality building materials to assist our customers to make the very best structures.

And the other one:

> Being efficient and speedy in our product delivery.

Now a possible combined statement may look like this:

Providing quality building materials efficiently and fast to assist our customers to make the very best structures.

The combined statement takes the best from both contributions. This joint statement reflects the thoughts of the two team members. Occasionally, one team member may be genuinely happy to adopt their colleague's statement without wanting to make any changes. This person may feel that the other statement captures their sentiments too. This is acceptable on the basis that both parties have had an input and finally agree that one contribution is best.

For a team of eight, for example, using this normative approach, you initially break up into four groups of two. Once these four pairs have come up with a joint declaration, you have whittled the purpose statement down to four contributions. In the case of odd numbers, one group of three is acceptable.

At any rate, from this initial step, each pair now joins another pair and repeats the process. Four people then share and discuss two statements. From this discussion, the aim is to end up with one purpose statement that the four support.

Once you have two statements, the team convenes and works with the two remaining statements to come up with one overall purpose statement. You'll be pleasantly surprised how well this collaboration works. Ultimately, your team will arrive at a purpose statement that everyone is invested in, in a reasonably short amount of time.

The word-smithing part of this exercise is important.

Finessing the language guarantees that the final words reflect the elements of a purpose statement I covered earlier in the chapter. "Words shape worlds."[46]

Take a moment to celebrate with the team on creating a team purpose statement. You have achieved a critical step in becoming a high-performing team. Congratulations.

In the next few steps, you'll run a similar process to identify the behaviors that support your team purpose.

What are the behaviors that will sustain the team's purpose? Without appropriate actions, all you have is a few words on a piece of paper. Unless the right behaviors match the purpose statement, nothing changes. If behaviors don't fit the team purpose, then it's a pointless process. And if nothing changes, team members are entitled to be cynical about purpose statements and their usefulness. That's why this next step is critical.

There's a difference between a *behavior* and an *attitude*. You will need to explain the difference between the two. An attitude is a state of mind, such as professionalism and cooperation. A behavior is a tangible manifestation of an attitude.

How is *professionalism* (attitude) demonstrated in behavioral terms, for instance? Two behaviors that support professionalism, for example, are *following through on promises to each other* and reviewing reports before sending them out to customers. How is *cooperation* (attitude) expressed as a tangible behavior? For *cooperation*, two behaviors might be *frequently asking colleagues if there is anything I can do to assist or speaking directly to the person whom you have a problem with in the first instance.*

Team members pair up again and select two attitudes

consistent with the team's purpose statement. Once pairs agree on two attitudes that support the purpose, invite them to share their response with the rest of the team. Encourage discussion on these attitudes.

Use the following questions to assist the conversation:

- *How* is the attitude defined?
- *What* are the behaviors consistent with this attitude?
- *How* do we know the behavior has been performed?
- *How* does the behavior help to achieve the team's purpose?
- *Where* should the behavior be applied in our work and interactions?
- *What* are the negative consequences if this behavior is neglected?
- *What* should we do if the attitude is violated?

These are good questions to discuss with the team to better understand the chosen attitudes and behaviors and their impact on team performance.

After identifying, discussing, and agreeing upon this information, you have created a *Team Purpose and Behavior Agreement*, consisting of a purpose statement and supporting attitudes and behaviors. The final step is to document this information for future reference.

Put it up as a poster (or several posters) around the work area to remind team members of their purpose and how it will be achieved. From time to time, you should challenge the work people do through the lens of team purpose and the accompanying behaviors. This document can also be used to affirm that the team is on track. Invite your colleagues to evaluate their own behavior and the behavior of others based on this agreement. You'll be pleasantly surprised at how effective this exercise is and its bearing on team performance.

In the next chapter, we discuss the next characteristic of bridging: managing stakeholders.

The top 10 key points

1. A team without a clear and compelling purpose gets side-tracked easily and frequently.

2. A team without purpose confuses busyness with achievement.

3. The team purpose and behavior agreement has two parts and is designed to facilitate a team purpose and set of guiding behaviors.

4. The team leader facilitates a dialog on the best way the team can work together.

5. Ask the team to reflect on these questions to begin with: What is our role as a team? What is our main goal? How should we define success? What benefits do we bring to our end-users or customers?

6. A good purpose statement is inspirational, expressed in a single sentence, focused on one key driver, concentrated on the end-user, and created collaboratively.

7. Take a moment to celebrate with the team on the creation of a team purpose statement.

8. Once the purpose statement has been created, the next step is to identify the behaviors that support

the team purpose.

9. The final step is to document the purpose statement and accompanying behaviors.

10. This document can also be used to affirm that the team is on track.

CHAPTER 15
Managing stakeholders

... when we make a genuine attempt to comprehend someone else's position, they'll often do the same with you.

Wendy and Ian, financial advisors working in the same team, simply couldn't agree on what direction to take. Both had their own version of what their client wanted and in which direction they should head.

Wendy was team leader. Ian had just joined her team from another area in the company. He brought with him a great reputation for managing stakeholders and clients.

The two met in the corridor after meeting their client to clarify the client's expectations. Both left the meeting believing they had a full and accurate understanding of the client's needs. They were surprised to discover that each had a different version of the meeting.

Wendy hadn't taken any notes during the meeting, relying instead on her prior knowledge of the client and the type of investment projects they were involved with. She had always felt comfortable dealing with this client, knowing their mood swings, values, and business very well.

Ian, on the other hand, being the newbie, had little background to go on and therefore had taken fast and furious notes during the meeting.

Wendy thought the client had approved her ideas and authorized the investment project to commence. Ian's impression was that the client wanted further financial options presented and that their decision to proceed would be based on additional costings being prepared and approved.

After several minutes of failing to convince each other of their differing perspectives of the meeting, Wendy and Ian stormed off to their offices, slamming the doors behind them in frustration.[47]

High-performing teams devote time to managing their stakeholders. It's hard to imagine a successful team having poor relations with its stakeholders. Managing stakeholders is the second characteristic in the Team Identity model associated with the bridging function.

A high-performing team does what's necessary to develop good productive working relationships with its key stakeholders. After all, a team's performance is ultimately dependent on working cooperatively with others outside the team. Managing stakeholders starts with an understanding of their motivation and influence on the team. Creating the right communication channels, setting clear mutual expectations, and juggling competing priorities are paramount for managing a team's stakeholders.

In this chapter, we'll look at the correct headspace a team needs to adopt to communicate effectively with those parties the team relies upon for information, cooperation, and support. The right mindset is particularly important when it's inevitable that conflicting priorities and differing perspectives will occur from time to time when dealing with an assortment of demanding stakeholders. In the next chapter, I'll share a stakeholder mapping exercise that's a useful starting point for managing stakeholders.

Managing stakeholders can be complex. Handling deadlines, for instance—when these priorities are often moving feasts—requires the ability to walk and chew gum at the same time. Mismanagement of deadlines, on the other hand, leads to misunderstanding, blame, mistrust, and frustration.

Mitigating stakeholder risk is another intricate issue—and by minimizing risk, it minimizes ulcers, too. And what about handling stakeholder interruptions that spoil a well-thought-out plan? How are these distractions curtailed or deflected? These are a few of the challenges a team inevitably encounters.

Effective stakeholder management also involves setting and managing the expectations others have of the team and what it can and can't deliver. More on that later.

Who are your stakeholders? Although it's a simple question, the answer isn't always obvious. A team has many stakeholders—more than it might initially appear. Most are easy to identify. But some of more obscure.

According to the *Association of Project Management*, stakeholder management is

> the systematic identification, analysis, planning, and implementation of actions to engage with stakeholders.[48]

Stakeholders can be individuals or groups—large and small—with a stake in a team task or project, or some connection directly or indirectly. Usually, stakeholders have a reciprocal pact with a team. Stakeholders, in varying degrees, have an impact on the team and vice versa.

Entities the team interacts with exert some form of influence over a team's performance, either constructively or destructively. They may be within or external to the team's organization, often both.

The senior management team is, for example, a powerful internal stakeholder group. Internal stakeholders, while generally easy to identify, are often overlooked or taken for granted.

External stakeholders can be disregarded too but can, nonetheless, have enormous influence over team performance and priority-setting. Government and its many agencies and tentacles, for instance, can exert pressure on the work of a team. Changes in priority, funding, and legislation, for example, affect a team and its priorities. But all stakeholders, wherever they are, and whoever they are, should be recognized, respected, and managed.

The exercise of identifying stakeholders must account for all individuals and groups that have any contact with a team. *Who are your forgotten stakeholders? How much influence do they really have? How can they influence the team?* are some questions that need to be considered. A team's customers and end-users are also affected by stakeholders.

Overlooked, a stakeholder can affect a team subtly and significantly. Neglected stakeholders could be managers, regulators, and specialists within or outside the organization. So, it is wise not to ignore a stakeholder.

What are your stakeholder's expectations? Are they

reasonable and realistic? What are your team's expectations of the stakeholder? These are also important questions that need addressing and monitoring throughout the duration of a team's working relationship. If it's a project relationship—with a finite start and finish date—ask the stakeholder early on how they'll measure success partnering with you.

It is inevitable that conflicts will arise occasionally. Stakeholder expectations can be flouted by a breach in process or outcome, or both. Process-driven expectations relate to procedures and protocol being followed and adhered to. Receiving update reports every third week of the month, for example, is a process-driven expectation. Outcome-driven expectations are based on the achievement of a result, for example, getting a project completed on time. In other words, some stakeholders will expect i's dotted and t's crossed (process-driven) while others just want "results" (outcome-driven), and others, still, want both.

Not all stakeholders are helpful and cooperative, alas. Some can be a pain in the backside to deal with. Others are a pleasure to work with. Most are somewhere in between these two extremes. Knowing early whether a stakeholder is likely to be an advocate or road-blocker is useful. You can then plan accordingly.

Road-blockers need close attention to minimize trouble.

- Why are they road blockers?
- Is the barrier task-related or personality-based?
- What do they need?
- What can the team do to mitigate the roadblock?

are questions worth pondering with your team.

Good teams either eliminate roadblocks, minimize them, or work around them.

Regardless of whether they are cooperative or not, engaging stakeholders as much as possible in the team's decision-making process, where it's appropriate, usually pays dividends. Also, ask for feedback. Communicate what the team is doing. Show appreciation. Make them feel important. Present information tailored to the way they do business, not the way your team does business. Be a useful resource to them and they may reciprocate and be useful to your team or, at least, not be a road-blocker. People generally treat you according to how you treat them.

Basic courtesy and respect—while underrated and in short supply—is the social lubricant. Stakeholders are naturally aware of the way you treat them. As difficult as it can be sometimes, be professional and polite in all your dealings. Be mindful that you will need them as much as they need you, if not more, at some stage. Stakeholders will judge you not only by what you do—or don't do—but by the way you do it. Manners matter.

These key points are worth considering. But managing stakeholders starts with understanding who they are and their association with the team. We are constantly being told to put ourselves in the shoes of others. This is harder than it sounds.

Can we *really* put ourselves in the shoes of someone else?

Anyway, there are broadly three perspectives we can choose to adopt when communicating with stakehold-ers—or anyone. These perspectives originate from Neuro-Linguistic Programming (NLP), popular since the

1970s.[49] NLP uses perceptual, behavioral, and communication techniques to make it easier for people to change their thoughts and actions.

Let's consider these three perspectives, referred to as first, second, and third position, and their application when communicating with stakeholders.

Figure 15.1 below illustrates these three positions.

Figure 15.1 The three-position model

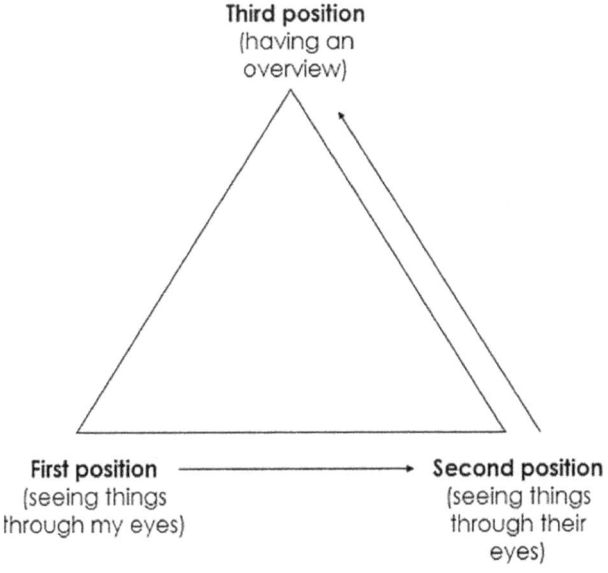

First position

First position is viewing the world through one's own eyes. As an illustration, consider being in a forest. If you are in the middle of a forest with your face pressed up against a large tree trunk, this is like first position. In first position, all you can see is what's directly in front of you—the tree trunk. With your head pushed up against a big tree, you can't see the other trees in the forest. If you didn't know better, you'd never know that you were in the middle of a tree-filled forest. Your vision in first position is short-sighted.

Although ineffective when communicating with others, first position is the position we are in most of the time. In first position, all we can see is what's in front of us. Our perspective is narrow and focused on one thing. In communication terms, that one thing is our own point of view.

Think of having a disagreement with someone. When that other person makes a statement you disagree with, you disregard it, while thinking only about your contrary poin –o -view. By defending your argument without considering the other person's argument, you are in first position. All you can "see" is your point-of-view, not theirs.

It's the easiest—and least helpful—position to adopt. Why? Because your energies are focused simply on your perspective. You aren't learning—or prepared to learn—anything new, just defending your turf in first position. You aren't prepared to take time and exert the energy necessary to consider their alternate perspective. Although you might have a good counter-argument, in first position, you aren't ready to explore their point of view. You are none the wiser about their view—although you may think you understand it implicitly.

So, when you see two people arguing with each other, they're both embracing first position in the model. Each person is passionately defending their viewpoint and not listening to the other. Finger-pointing. Raised voices. Eyeballing. These are all visual illustrations of first position.

From a stakeholder management perspective, first position is also the least helpful of the three positions. Taking this stance, a team member vigorously defends their position. The team member(s) isn't considering the perspective of the stakeholder, regardless of its legitimacy. And quite probably in response, the stakeholder isn't taking into consideration the team's position, either.

Where the rubber meets the road

Looking at the issue through your eyes

This is a common mistake that can easily occur at the outset of an engagement process, with even the best intentions. We're hard-wired to view things through our own eyes (first position), and as a result, even good leaders can make the wrong assumptions about how a decision will impact their stakeholders, based on their own unique lens on the world and what they believe to be true.

It isn't a character flaw—it's human nature. As leaders, we often have a unique and even privileged view of an issue. What's important to remember, though, is it isn't always the only view.

Stakeholder mapping—the process of identifying and categorizing all your stakeholder groups—is a proven method used by successful teams. They know that engaging their diverse community early in the process—even inviting the community to help identify

> and define the issue—allows them to see through many eyes. True insight may be defined as being able to view an issue (or opportunity) from the perspectives of as diverse a group as possible.[50]

Second position

Second position is a more effective communication position to take with stakeholders, or anyone else.

Getting back to the forest analogy, second position is like stepping back from the tree trunk you had your face pressed against. By taking a step back from the tree, you now see that you're in a forest—the tree you were facing is one of thousands of trees that make up a large ecosystem.

Second position means putting yourself into a place where you can understand a perspective other than your own. People are not always capable or willing, however, to put themselves in second position.

So, if you are arguing with someone who has a different opinion to you, you can shift to second position, as challenging as it sometimes is. What this means is that you try to comprehend their counterview. You stop defending your position for a moment and ask them to elaborate on their position, so you can fully grasp where they are coming from.

Why do this if you are right, or at least think you are right? Well, remember this: the person you are having a disagreement with thinks they are right, too! By completely understanding their perspective, you expand your outlook beyond your own. This is like standing back from the tree to see other parts of the forest. In second position, you can potentially understand the other person's opinion or position.

After listening to their argument, you may not agree with what they're saying. But at least you know why they disagree.

Interestingly, when we make a genuine attempt to comprehend someone else's position, they'll often do the same with you. Adopting second position can, in other words, encourage the other person to listen to your argument, too. You could end up "agreeing to disagree," but at least you appreciate their circumstances more fully. Occasionally, in second position, you may be won over by their argument, or vice versa.

This is a more constructive position to be in with a stakeholder who holds a different stance to the team. And let's face it: stakeholders often do have a dissimilar perspective. Wouldn't it be useful to at least understand why they have a disparate view to your own?

Third position

Third position in the model is the superior perspective. In third position, you still have a point of view and willingly defend it (first position). Additionally, you appreciate a differing point of view and understand the arguments for why the stakeholder has adopted it (second position). In third position, you can also grasp the context and other contingency factors impacting on the issue of disagreement.

Getting back to the forest analogy, third position is like getting into a helicopter and flying over the forest you once inhabited. You now see the forest in its entirety. You can't see the individual trees, but you can see the full landscape. You have an overview or helicopter view.

Recall the two people arguing in first position. After

understanding the other person's perspective by listening (second position), they now consider the range of factors that influence the issue. This is adopting third position.

You can appreciate the driving and restraining forces at play that impact the differing points of view in third position. The dispute is viewed and understood in the context of the bigger picture. Third position enables you to view the variance of viewpoint in the milieu of circumstances impacting this disagreement. Isn't that a better and more constructive position to be in?

Being in third position can be summed up in two words: *political awareness*. People who are politically savvy readily assume a third position on complex issues. They may still have strong and unwavering beliefs and arguments and can empathize with competing views. Further, they can see the problem in the context of the surrounding environment. A politically aware leader has a tactical advantage.

When dealing with stakeholders, third position is the most exceptional communication position of the three. A high-performing team is aware of its surroundings. It therefore has the capability to develop useful ways to navigate through differing perspectives. The politically aware team has the wherewithal to construct bridges between their interests and the interests of others working with the team.

However, many business practices discourage people and teams from espousing a third position. The Western legal system is adversarial, for example. There is usually a winner and a loser. Occasionally, there are two losers and two winners—but rarely. Our political system consists of a government and opposition—both parties adopt a confrontational stance. Sometimes they collaborate or act in a bipartisan matter, but that's the exception rather than the rule. So third position is not necessarily a natural position.

Nonetheless, shifting one's mindset from first to second and third position is an advantage in our "win-lose" culture. If a lawyer can understand the competitor's position more clearly and appreciate the context of the case, for example, they can mount a stronger argument for their client. The lawyer, assuming a third position, can ponder a wide array of issues and pressures that are brought to bear on their client's circumstances. They can then plan a more sophisticated strategy to navigate the terrain.

By shifting to second position and better understanding an opposition's argument, a political party can potentially dismantle its argument. Better still, by moving to third position, the party can contemplate various pressure groups and their motivations on the issue at stake. This helicopter view may provide sufficient awareness to enable them to find a way through the maze to win the day.

All told, even though society perpetuates a first position mentality, it is expedient to rise above this prevailing mindset (like the helicopter view of the forest) and assume a third position.

We've considered the value of stakeholder management in this chapter. Developing good communication channels with an interested party can benefit any team. Stakeholder management is one of two characteristics associated with the bridging function of team identity.

In the next chapter, we explore an exercise in stakeholder mapping.

The top 10 key points

1. High-performing teams devote time to managing their stakeholders

2. Effective stakeholder management involves setting and managing the expectations others have of the team and what it can and can't deliver.

3. Stakeholder management is the systematic identification, analysis, planning, and implementation of actions to engage with stakeholders.

4. Regardless of whether they are cooperative or not, engaging stakeholders as much as possible in the team's decision-making process, where it's appropriate, usually pays dividends.

5. There are broadly three perspectives we can choose to adopt when communicating with stakeholders—or anyone.

6. First position is viewing the world through one's own eyes.

7. Although ineffective when communicating with others, first position is the position we are in most of the time.

8. Second position means putting yourself into a place where you can understand a perspective other than your own.

9. In third position, you can also grasp the context and other contingency factors impacting on the issue of disagreement.

10. All told, even though society perpetuates a first position mentality, it is expedient to rise above this prevailing mindset (like the helicopter view of the forest) and assume a third position.

CHAPTER 16

Mapping stakeholders using the SPIR model

Managing stakeholders is everyone's responsibility, not just the team leader's.

In this chapter, I'll explain the SPIR model and how it can be used to manage stakeholders. SPIR is designed to prioritize a team's top five stakeholders in a systematic way. By mapping stakeholders and understanding their impact and influence on team success, you have consciously shifted to third position—the concept we discussed in the last chapter.

Aside from being methodical, SPIR is intended to be a collaborative exercise, with full team participation. By involving everyone in this exercise, SPIR serves two useful purposes. First, it draws on the collective wisdom of the team. Many heads are better than one, as they say. Second, by including all team members in the discussion, awareness of stakeholder management is enhanced. The team is therefore likely to commit to building better, more productive stakeholder relationships.

Managing stakeholders is everyone's responsibility, not just the team leader's.

So, how does the SPIR exercise work?

The leader starts by drawing a circle in the middle of a large whiteboard and writes the words our team in the circle. Team members are then asked to identify all the stakeholders they deal with or are likely to deal with in the future. Aim for at least 10 stakeholders. Write the stakeholders' names on the board with a two-way arrow to the circle in the middle to signify a reciprocal communication channel.

The list should include stakeholders within the organization and external to the organization. Stakeholders can be individuals, teams, or entities. A stakeholder might be Mary Johnston in accounts or the dispatch team (internal), for example, or an industry association (external). For an entity such as a government agency or membership association, it's useful to identify the key contact(s) you liaise with in that group.

SPIR model

SPIR is short for *Stake, Power, Importance*, and *Regularity*. Each of these words represents a significant criterion for assessing a stakeholder's value to the team. These labels cover the following principles:

- Stake—the stakeholder's financial, emotional, or reputational stake in the team's success.

- Power—the influence the stakeholder has over the team's ability to achieve its purpose.

- Importance—the team's reliance on the stakeholder for resources.

- Regularity—the regularity of contact with the stakeholder.

Once all stakeholders have been identified and recorded on the whiteboard—with key contacts—go back and discuss and rate each on a scale of 1 to 5 (5 = high and 1= low) for each criterion.

Here are the guidelines for evaluation.

Stake

Stake refers to the extent of the stakeholder's vested interest in the team's success. If you rate a stakeholder a 5, it's because the stakeholder has a significant financial, emotional, or reputational stake in your team's achievements.

For example, if you're a sales team, the sales director (internal stakeholder) has a high stake in the performance of the team. The sales director will expect regular reports and updates on sales activity. What's more, their reputation will be boosted or tarnished based on the team's sales volume. Based on the stake criteria, the sales director will rate a 5.

At the other end of the scale, a team supplier external to the organization may not have much of a stake in team performance. Your team could be one of hundreds of teams that this stakeholder supplies across the world. Their stake may, for example, rate a 1 because of the high number of organizations to which they supply product.

Consider the extent of each stakeholder's interest in your team's success.

Where the rubber meets the road

The Evolution of Influence

The word influence comes from the Latin word influ-ere, which means "to flow into." In the late fourteenth century, an astrological connection continued with the word being defined as "streaming ethereal power from the stars acting upon character or destiny of men." Later, in the fifteenth century, the word evolved into a closer version of today's definition, "exercise of personal power by human beings," and in the 1580s, the meaning became "exertion of unseen influence by persons." As a point of reference, the term "under the influence," as it relates to being intoxicated, first appeared in 1866!

Today, the Merriam-Webster Dictionary defines influence as the power or capacity to cause an effect in indirect or intangible ways. The Oxford Dictionary has a similar definition, stating that influence is the capacity to affect the character, development, or behavior of someone or something, or the effect itself.

John C. Maxwell, an author, speaker, and internationally recognized leadership expert, is quoted as saying "leadership is influence." Once we expand that quote, we can clearly see how important it is for managers to have the skills and expertise to elicit the best from their employees and co-workers.[51]

Power

A stakeholder's power to influence a team can vary considerably. Power over the team can be exerted in several ways. In their research, social psychologists John French and Bertrand Raven classified several power bases.[52] The table below illustrates power as either *positional* or *personal*.

Table 16.1 Powerbases

Positional power	Personal power
Legitimate power	Referent power
Coercive power	Expert power
Reward power	Connection power
Information power	

In the organizational structure, positional power is based on hierarchical status. The CEO exerts more power than the janitor, for instance. Personal power, on the other hand, is derived from someone's personal qualities, rather than the position they hold. A construction team may seek advice on a project from an engineer because of their expertise in building, for instance. Positional and personal power can be exerted by a stakeholder.

Here is a brief explanation of each source of power listed in Table 16.1, commencing with positional powerbases.

Legitimate power

Titles and positions denote organizational status. If you're *head of department*, for instance, people in your department will regularly submit to your judgment because of the position you hold.

Legitimate power doesn't, however, carry the same

weight it once did—people are generally not as impressed by one's title or position anymore. People in positions of legitimate power, such as police officers and teachers, for example, cannot rely on their authority to the same extent they once did.

Nonetheless, a team liaising with someone who exercises legitimate power can get things done relatively easily, assuming, of course, it has a good working relationship with them. Cultivating positive relationships with the titleholder in a stakeholder organization is wise.

Coercive power

Coercive power is founded on fear. It'd be a mistake to assume that the execution of coercive power is less prevalent today. Fear is—and probably always will be—an effective short-term motivator. Physical coercion is rarely used anymore by stakeholders unless it's the Mafia! There are laws in place to prevent a beating or a threat of a beating in the workplace.

But psychological coercion is still rife. Stakeholders can and do exert psychological coercion in a variety of ways. The withdrawal or the threat of withdrawing support, for example, can be done by simply ignoring or not responding to an email. Threatening a team or its leader with scrutiny by a regulatory authority is another form of psychological coercion. These tactics are not uncommon, and may even be on the rise.

Reward power

Reward power is the opposite of coercive power. Rewards such as special favors or incentives can be a powerful inducement. Offering useful information, attendance at special functions, access to influential decision-makers, and so on, are examples of the exercising of reward power.

Stakeholders in the private sector probably have more scope to administer these kinds of overt incentives than public sector stakeholders, who are bound by more regulations. Nevertheless, public sector stakeholders still administer rewards, but perhaps not to the same extent.

Recognition is another form of reward power—it could range from a simple thank-you through to nominating an enterprising team for a prestigious reward. The capacity to publicly recognize the good work of a team is a form of influence exercised by some stakeholder groups.

Information power

Using privileged information to change someone's opinion or behavior is another form of positional power. People who hold high-status positions, such as CEO, can have access to important information before others. (Sometimes they can be the last to know, too!) However, access to useful information means it can either be conveyed to or withheld from groups or individuals, depending upon the intent of the informant.

If someone in power has advance notice of a policy change or new legislation, they can disclose this information to the team's advantage. The receiver of this information can make plans and start preparations, gaining a head start over rivals. Certain changes in taxation or superannuation laws can, for example, be communicated to a financial services institution from a government agency in the know. Armed with this information, the business can make the necessary adjustments to gain a competitive advantage in the marketplace, notwithstanding the ethics of doing so.

Knowledge is power is the basis of this power source.

These four powerbases come from the privilege of position. Now let's consider the dimension of personal power.

Referent power

Referent power is based on one's personal attributes. People who possess referent power are respected and admired by others because of their engaging personality. Some may call this *charisma*.

People follow others who are charismatic because they have a certain kind of magnetism or appeal. This attraction can result in direct or indirect influence over others.

Direct referent power is persuading others by force of personality. Indirect influence may come by being a role model or exemplar to others who are impressionable to the sway of that leader. A junior team member wants to emulate their team leader's leadership style and approach, for example, although the leader may be unaware of their influence on the young person.

Expert power

Sought-after expertise, skill, or knowledge is the foundation of expert power. We refer to lawyers for legal matters, psychologists for psycho-emotional problems, IT professionals for technology issues, and so on. These experts have extensive knowledge and skills in a narrow, sought-after field. In circumstances where someone needs what an expert has to offer, they can exert influence.

All teams rely on stakeholders for expertise either

regularly or intermittently. For example, a construction team needs the town planning department for approval of their plans. Within an organization, a human resource manager proficient in conflict resolution or a seasoned manager mentoring new managers are examples of those who can be consulted for advice by a team. Whether it's skills or experience, people who have know-how that others may benefit from can exercise expert power.

Connection Power

Lastly, connection power stems from having access to valuable contacts. By having many useful connections, one can draw upon these people to get things done. By calling upon the skills and expertise of others, having connections is a form of borrowed power. Politicians trade on connections; for example, they cultivate important contacts in their local communities and call upon these people when needed.

Stakeholders who have wide-ranging connections can be a valuable resource to the team in certain circumstances. A professional association has access to a large body of professionals, such as accountants. Access to this professional body would be valuable for a team looking to recruit an accountant, for example.

Discuss the powerbases of each stakeholder.

- What sort of positional and personal power does a stakeholder possess that may help or hinder our team?

- What rating out of five would we give each stakeholder based on their powerbases?

are questions to consider.

Importance

Importance in the model refers to the extent to which the team relies on the stakeholder to accomplish its purpose. Is the stakeholder critical or peripheral to team success?

The level of importance a team gives its stakeholder for its success isn't always reciprocated. Your team may rely extensively on a stakeholder's input and support to get its work done. However, that stakeholder may not view your team as a high priority. This type of arrangement can potentially be problematic for your team. In this situation—where the stakeholder is critical for team performance but doesn't view the team with the same importance—the team needs to give special attention to that stakeholder.

Teams depend on stakeholders in various ways. Support can be financial, informational, educational, or instructional. From a financial perspective, senior management (internal stakeholder) can cut, increase, or maintain the annual budget of the team. Stakeholders can provide information that's valuable for a team. It might be a customer service survey report written by an independent external consultant on the team's strengths and opportunities for growth, for example, that can assist a team to improve its performance. Suppliers to a team, such as the internal IT department, can offer training and coaching to use the technology more efficiently and effectively. A government agency can offer advice on navigating the system's red tape. All these services and support are valuable for team accomplishment.

When rating each stakeholder in terms of their level of importance, consider these questions:

- What can this stakeholder offer the team?

- If they decided to withdraw their support, what would be the consequences?

Then rate the stakeholder's importance on a scale of 1 to 5.

Regularity

Finally, *regularity* is concerned with the frequency of interaction between the team and the stakeholder. Is it daily, weekly, monthly, or yearly? Regularity of contact should be considered in the stakeholder assessment for good reason. Daily contact, for instance, suggests a high degree of reliance on a stakeholder and, perhaps, vice versa. The manager of the team leader would be an example of regular, daily contact. At the other end of the spectrum, a government regulator may have contact with the team once a year for reporting or statutory purposes.

It stands to reason that the more frequent the contact, the more important it is to foster a good working relationship with that stakeholder. But it's easy to take for granted a stakeholder whom the team has regular contact with, even though it is very reliant on them.

Now rate your stakeholders in terms of regularity of contact. The more frequent, the higher the score. Daily contact would rate a 5, weekly a 4, and so on, through to 1 for annual contact.

It's time to tally the four scores (Stake, Power, Importance, and Regularity) for each stakeholder. Discuss and calculate the scores on the map. Identify the top five stakeholders, based on the scores for the SPIR criteria.

Once you have established your top five stakeholders, discuss with the team ways of developing better working relationships with each. Here are some questions to guide the conversation:

- What can we do in the limited time we have to cement better working relationships with this stakeholder?
- How will we do this?
- Who in the team will be responsible for this? One or all?

Then go to work to manage your high-priority stakeholders. The effort will pay off. This, of course, doesn't mean ignoring the other stakeholders. But by prioritizing the top five connections the team has, you have developed a focus on managing key stakeholders.

In the next chapter, we look at the first characteristic of the building strategy: improving systems.

The top 10 key points

1. SPIR is short for Stake, Power, Importance, and Regularity.

2. Stake refers to the extent to which the stakeholder has a vested interest in the team's success.

3. Stakeholders' power to influence a team will vary considerably.

4. There are two dimensions of power: positional and personal.

5. Positional power could be legitimate, coercive, reward, or informational.

6. Personal power covers three types: referent, expert, or connection.

7. Importance refers to the extent to which the team relies on the stakeholder.

8. Regularity of contact should be considered in the assessment.

9. Tally the four scores (Stake, Power, Importance, and Regularity) for each stakeholder and identify the top five stakeholders.

10. Discuss with the team ways of developing superior working relationships with the top five stakeholders.

CHAPTER 17
Improving systems

Winning teams become losing teams when they become satisfied with the status quo.

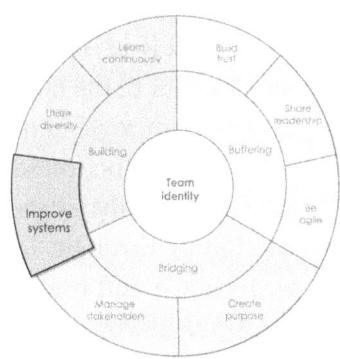

"**W**e're always challenging the status quo," *says All Black coach Graham Henry. "Always challenging the way we do things, both as an individual and as a team—how can we do things better?" One of the pillars of the All Black environment is that it's devoted to learning—the management are students of the game, constantly looking for the edge.*[53]

Improving systems is the first of three characteristics supporting the building function of team identity. Building involves constructing a productive and sustainable team culture. Improving systems is defined, its main barrier is discussed, and opportunities for continuous improvement are considered in this chapter.

Without continually improving the way it carries out its work, a team will struggle to uphold its relevance in a world of relentless change and mounting ambiguity. Successful teams, like the All Blacks, periodically question their systems and processes. Constructive reflection is part of a high-performing team's DNA. Winning teams aren't complacent and comfortable in the belief they have nothing to learn or improve. Winning teams become losing teams when they become satisfied with the status quo. To stay ahead of the curve, good teams find time to contemplate their processes, systems, and procedures. Nothing a team does is off-limits. It's all open to scrutiny. Successful teams strive to be better, faster, and more successful, all the time.

Improving systems puts the spotlight squarely on continuous development and modification. As I've said several times so far, particularly in CHAPTER 11, there's lots of fuss now about the need to be agile. But in the hurly-burly of work, too little time is found for improvement conversations. With a fixation on job specification, these discussions—when they do occur—are usually afterthoughts, done superficially, with no follow-through. In the next chapter, I will discuss a well-known and useful (if not well-practiced) methodology for reviewing work practices.

Discussing ways to produce and do team tasks better, faster, and more easily is often glossed over in team reviews—if there's any review at all! There's little or no time allocated to discussing fresh ideas and advances—it's not usually considered a high priority. But there always seems to be oodles of time to talk about problems and apportion blame when things go wrong. Employees are understandably left with the impression that doing their job well, according to their job description, is all that counts. Working *in the team* and not *on the team* is the norm.

Process improvement takes a back seat to achieving immediate outcomes. Continuously improving the team's processes doesn't get the attention it deserves. Questions such as *How can we do things faster/with fewer errors/with reduced costs/with higher quality/with more customer responsiveness?* aren't usually asked, let alone satisfactorily answered.

Employees are taught to follow standard systems and processes, told to hit KPIs consistently, and expected to obey directions. This leaves little scope for original thought or enterprise. Team members then, unsurprisingly, become complacent—they aren't encouraged to think about or explore team improvements. Instead of being the pilot flying the plane, team members are the passengers on the flight.

A mindset of stability, predictability, and certainty

Most people at work are still locked into the 20th century mindset of stability, predictability, and certainty. This conservative attitude inhibits creative thinking and continuous improvement. Managers set up systems, processes, and procedures and expect employees to follow them without question. The rationalization for a system is that it's the one best way of accomplishing an activity or task. Followers are praised for following standard practice and criticized—even punished—for not doing so. With this straight-jacket mentality, it's tough to improve existing systems and workflow.

Despite this prevailing mentality, people are still confused about what to do, or not do. On the one hand, employees are expected to follow normal operating procedures. On the other hand, they're expected to be enterprising—to display initiative in certain situations. That's a hard juggling act. Therefore, the default position taken when put in the predicament of displaying initiative or being compliant is to take the easy path. And that path is to faithfully observe orthodox work practices—it's less risky and considered the safest route.

But warp speed change calls for the enterprise route to be taken more and more. The challenge facing the 21st century team is like playing a tennis match both left- and right-handed—to be both unadventurous and enterprising. This is what Charles O'Reilly and Michael Tushman coin the *ambidextrous organization*.[54] According to the authors, survival and success depend on the ability to be ambidextrous.

To be ambidextrous, teams need to have a dual focus on adhering to standard practice and showing initiative. But unleashing the enterprising talents of people and their potential to think with freedom is tough against a backdrop of specialization and systemization.

An overreliance on formulaic practices is essentially about control. Conformity is easy to measure and monitor. Employee performance can be objectively evaluated against a set criterion, namely, a KPI. We live in a world fixated with models, targets, KPIs, and QA. By designing work and assessing people against a series of KPIs, the manager simplifies and standardizes production. Further, assessing and judging people's work can be justified as objective and fair, even in a VUCA environment.[55]

So, from a manager's perspective, it's easier to assess whether someone is following a system than assessing whether a system is improved. And from a team member's point of view, it's easier to follow a system than question its relevance and application.

When discussing the characteristic of sharing leadership in CHAPTER 9, I categorized decision-making three ways.

Here's a brief recap.

Some decisions are black and white. In these situations, the right response is to follow the system without hesitation. Most decisions around safety, compliance, and government regulatory requirements spring to mind, for instance.

Conversely, some decisions call for an original solution. For example, a truck driver delivering products to a customer may notice that the business is short-staffed at the time of delivery. Although not conventional, instead of immediately moving off to the next delivery after unloading the merchandise, he elects to help his customer store the product in the warehouse. This is likely to be appreciated by the receiving company and generates goodwill, strengthening the possibility for future orders for the driver's firm.

The third type of decision is a Catch-22: *Do I follow the rules, or do I show initiative?* This category—which is neither black and white nor blue sky—is where decision-making is tested. In these grey areas, the safest route is to follow due process, even when displaying initiative—with its associated risks—could attain a superior result.

For example, Greta is in charge of purchasing bulk product in a team with stringent purchasing rules and regulations. One of those policies is to order the product on the last day of each month. Greta has heard from a reliable source that her team has won a large contract with a new customer. This customer requires immediate delivery of a large order. She decides to order outside the normal ordering cycle in anticipation of this new customer's needs. Greta's enterprising behavior violates the team's purchasing policy; it's nevertheless in the interests of the new customer to do so and, ultimately, in the interests of her team and company too.

Not everyone thinks—or is encouraged to think—like Greta. Most employees fail to be proactive in this kind of situation and tow the party line. But it's in these scenarios—where things aren't inevitably straightforward—that leaders struggle to encourage prudent initiative from others. These types of challenges and their potential solutions should be discussed in team meetings, preferably before deciding, but, at the very least, after the event as a learning opportunity. Whether briefing or debriefing, the team can agree upon what ought to be done now and in similar future circumstances. These discussions build confidence and promote initiative.

Where the rubber meets the road

A random act of kindness

Talking about improving systems—there aren't too many more systemized industries than the airline industry. But this story I read of a Southwest pilot takes the prize for initiative!

On September 11, 2001, a certain pilot didn't feel hamstrung by following a system. This is what could be termed a random *act of kindness*—one that left an indelible impression on everyone on his flight.

Like all aircraft pilots flying on that fateful day, he was instructed to land at the nearest airport. He appropriately followed this directive. But when the plane landed, he did something extraordinary.

He followed normal protocol in the event of a grounded plane, making sure that everyone was accounted for and safely ensconced at the designated hotel. But he went further. This pilot chose to entertain everyone on his flight with a night out at the local cinema during an event of great uncertainty and panic.[56]

Where to start?

Where should you start improving your team's systems? Start with the everyday routine processes of the team. Often, when leaders are challenged to be innovative, they freeze. *Where do I start?* they think. Start on the conventional and mundane tasks.

- What mandatory team activities chew up a lot of time, with little result?
- What systems can be changed?
- What might make a difference?

Ask your team—involve them in a discussion.

Here's another suggestion: Ask people to audit their time for three days. On analyzing their time usage, it'll give a clear and accurate indication of the activities that take the most time and involve the most people. If everyone is expected to follow a system or process, such as writing reports—the activity absorbing the bulk of team time—then this may be a good place to start. Why? A small improvement in an approach that's used regularly can reap a big difference in efficiency or effectiveness.

Every individual, team, organization, and industry prospers from streamlining their routine work. Therefore, it's worth making this a priority for improvement. Systems won't change without three deliberate steps:

1. Create the time and space to examine systems

2. Initiate a conversation about how systems can be improved and

3. Involve those affected by the system.

A systems improvement conversation can be done one-on-one or with the whole team. Its purpose is to explore ways to make the system more efficient and effective.

Key improvement questions to consider are:

- How can this process be done more *quickly*?

- How can this process be done more *accurately*?

- How can this activity be done in a *timelier* manner?

- How can this procedure be carried out more *cost*-effectively?

- How can this task be done with greater *productivity*?

Apart from building upon what's already in place, the improving systems conversation can also consider replacing an old system with a new system. It could even include abandoning a system entirely. This examination includes systems used between the team and external sources too. The bottom line is this: Everything that's done within a team should be examined, with the purpose of improvement.

Improving systems shouldn't discount the possibility of coming up with an entirely new way of doing something (innovation). As defined in CHAPTER 11, continuous improvement is about how to build upon what we already have—whereas innovation asks: *Is there a new way?* Briefly, continuous improvement is improving the current state, and innovation is transforming the current state. Improving systems covers both possibilities.

Where the rubber meets the road

Online tombstone inscriptions

Several years ago, a local government authority was aware of the growing number of complaints it received from the public. Specifically, these complaints were about the length of time taken to get tombstone inscriptions completed in time for a funeral. The current process was cumbersome.

A relative of the deceased would draft the details to appear on the tombstone and send them off to the relevant council department. The department would subsequently complete a draft and send it back to the relative for approval. Once the member of the public had signed off on the wording and design, the council officer would then have the tombstone inscribed. This process took two weeks to complete.

Relatives of the deceased became understandably upset and distressed at the length of time this procedure took, particularly when they wanted to complete the burial. This method was unwieldy, requiring several checks back and forward between members of the public and council staff. It became apparent that an entirely new system was needed.

The challenge was to find a better way to speed up this approval process while being 100 percent accurate with the tombstone transcription. An online solution was devised. In a newly created section of the council's website, the relative of the deceased would complete the wording they wanted on the tombstone. The officer could immediately do a draft copy and send it back to the relative electronically for checking. Once the relative was happy with the draft, the officer commenced the engraving. This reduced the process from two weeks to one week. This new method is now common practice.[57]

Once an idea has been floated in the team, assessing its viability is the next important step.

Assessing ideas

Here are some guidelines you might find useful for assessing the merits of an idea raised. The criteria are based on three practical considerations—*time, complexity*, and *cost*.

Time

How long will it take to implement the idea? The less time the better, of course. Ideas that take months or years to realize are going to be less appealing and more challenging. Concepts that can be applied immediately are going to be more attractive because they're less intrusive. These simple solutions are the low-hanging fruit.

Complexity

By complexity, I'm referring to the potential drain on resources. *How much impact will the idea have on the team's resources?* These resources cover administrative, technical, and human. More specifically,

- What systems and processes need changing to make the idea work (administrative)?
- Does the current technology support the idea (technical)?
- Who and how will people be affected by the change (human)?

The less complex the idea, the easier its implementation is likely to be.

Cost

Cost of implementation must be factored into the assessment of a new systems approach. A cost-benefit analysis needs to be thought out, if not documented.

- What are the costs of applying the idea?
- What benefits are envisaged?

Cost is sometimes difficult to quantify. Also, it's

sometimes hard to assess—or even anticipate—the benefits accurately. You need to nonetheless weigh up the idea in terms of whether the benefits offset the costs or vice versa.

In summary, the time the idea takes to come to fruition, the degree of difficulty, and the impact upon team resources need to be assessed. A decision on the concept's feasibility can then be made with some confidence. An idea that takes considerable time and is complex and costly shouldn't necessarily be discounted, however. If the return is predicted to be momentous in terms of

- quality improvement
- savings in overall costs and time and
- increases in output and safety,

then it might be worthwhile, with more attention.

A more thorough feasibility study or cost-benefit analysis may be warranted as the next step.

The criteria of time, complexity, and cost provide you with a simple analytical framework for evaluating change. If the upside is more appealing than the downside, then the execution of the idea can be defensible.

In the next chapter, we explore the After-action Review and its application to systems review.

The top 10 key points

1. Improving systems is the first of three characteristics supporting the building function of team identity.

2. Most people at work are still locked into the 20th century mindset of stability, predictability, and certainty. This conservative attitude inhibits creative thinking and continuous improvement.

3. Where should you start improving your team's systems? Start with the everyday routine processes of the team.

4. Systems won't change without three deliberate actions: creating the time and space to examine systems; initiating a conversation about how they can be improved; and involving those affected by the system.

5. Apart from building upon what's already in place, the improving systems conversation can also consider replacing an old system with a new system.

6. Once an idea has been floated, assessing its viability is the next important step.

7. One criterion for assessing the viability of an idea is the time it takes for implementation.

8. A second criterion for assessing an idea is its complexity.

9. A third criterion is cost.

10. An idea that takes considerable time and is complex and costly shouldn't necessarily be discounted.

CHAPTER 18
Refining systems using the After-action Review

The Army's After-action Review is arguably one of the most successful organizational learning methods yet devised.

Debriefing and feedback are important to the All Blacks' success. In the All Blacks' feedback-rich culture, transparency is encouraged. The amount of discussion on performance is far greater than the standard practice of other sporting teams.

Individually and collectively, the All Blacks maintain a running commentary on performance as it occurs.

They invest in learning from today to help them become better tomorrow. The All Blacks learn from every training session and every game, regardless of whether they win, lose, or draw.

Improving the team's systems can be done in a variety of ways. One reputable and highly effective way—although underused in the corporate world—is the After-action Review (AAR). Getting the necessary information on whether a system is working optimally requires feedback. Timely feedback during or immediately after the completion of a project or task is preferable to delaying the review, or not doing it at all. We consider the AAR as a tool for feedback and review in this chapter.

Systems feedback can be positive or negative, or a bit of both. Positive feedback on a system reinforces its current practice. Negative feedback suggests that corrective action is necessary to improve the system. This feedback should happen continuously (formative feedback) or at the end (summative) of a project.

Intermittent debriefing meetings (formative feedback) give a team the opportunity to ask questions to elicit relevant information during a project. This feedback can lead to systems improvement throughout a project. An end-of-project debrief (formative feedback) can produce useful information for business development for the next project. Both vehicles of feedback have their merits for process changes.

Either way, everyone in the team must be invited to provide feedback, as the All Blacks do. Feedback on the team's systems, processes, and procedures should be part of that feedback cycle. The prime purpose of systems feedback is to improve the way a team goes about its business.

System reviews

If systems aren't reviewed, there's little likelihood of their changing for the better. Reviewing systems can be done in four ways. Table 18.1 below summarizes these four options.

Table 18.1 Systems review options

Formative	Summative	
Regular dialog	End-of-project debrief	Informal
Check-in	End-of-project report	Formal

In the above table, a formative review is done recurrently. A summative review is done at the end of the project. On the right-hand side, an informal review refers to an ad hoc, spontaneous approach. A formal review is a set and structured review. This provides four options for reviewing work processes: *Regular dialog* and *Check-in* (Formative)and *End-of-project debrief* and *End-of-project report* (Summative).

Let's briefly consider each option for reviewing systems.

Regular dialog

Regular dialog is reviewing systems frequently and casually. This form of appraisal would happen where a leader works alongside others during a team project. On the spur of the moment, the leader can challenge the way the team is carrying out its tasks. By raising questions on the spot, the leader, seizing the moment, challenges colleagues to critique the way something is being done. This could be done individually or collectively during or after an activity. Through these regular casual conversations, this system review option discusses what is working and what's not.

Check-in

A check-in also means regular reviewing but doing so in a more structured and systematic way. This might be a set series of frequent, formal review meetings throughout a project. Regular check-ins are useful when there's some project complexity, with many stakeholders and an assortment of systems and processes. In these circumstances, a more structured, ongoing feedback process is apt.

End-of-project debrief

The end-of-project debrief is a flexible appraisal at the completion of a project. This kind of review is suitable for simple projects where participants have a thorough understanding of the tasks involved. In these situations, the leader can facilitate a conversation with a free-flowing exchange of ideas on various aspects of the project process and its outcome.

End-of-project report

Lastly, the end-of-project report, as its name implies, is also carried out once a project has been finished, but is done formally, either in a written or verbal format. This review option occurs when the leader wants to formally assess specific processes and procedures to guide and inform decision-making for subsequent projects. These reports follow a set structure.

For the two summative approaches in Table 18.1, the main purpose is to apply lessons learned for similar projects in the future. Since this feedback is done at the end of a project, its purpose is to improve team efficiencies and effectiveness from lessons learned. For the end-of-project debrief, a leader gains consensus from the team on improvements moving forward. A project report, being more formal, can make recommendations to be applied in future planning. By documenting the recommendations, they are available for future reference.

The two formative approaches in Table 18.1 are more suited to making immediate modifications and changes during a project. Regular dialog is more suited to making ad hoc changes, and regular check-ins are designed to review segments of work in the project cycle. Both options facilitate incremental change.

Whichever review option is used, the AAR can be applied.

After-action Review

According to management guru Peter Senge in *The Dance of Change*:

> The Army's After-action Review (AAR) is arguably one of the most successful organizational learning methods yet devised. Yet, most every corporate effort to graft this truly innovative practice into their culture has failed because, again and again, people reduce the living practice of AAR to a sterile technique.[58]

High praise indeed.

What exactly is an AAR?

The AAR is a debriefing methodology that shares lessons from the past to make enhancements for the future. AARs are applicable in any review process. They can be done during or at the completion of any project. Further, an AAR can be used informally or formally. Its practice is versatile and can be employed to improve systems or anything else that is open to enhancement.

The spirit of the AAR is based on openness and learning—it's not a tool for apportioning blame or finding fault. Lessons learned can be shared on the spot or documented and shared with a wider audience.

The AAR was originally developed—and is still extensively used—by the US Army. The business world has been slow to appreciate its value and adopt this tool in its workplaces. And unfortunately, many organizations that have adopted the AAR use it as a quality check, rather than as a continuous improvement methodology. Using the AAR as a box-ticking exercise diminishes its power.

What makes the AAR so effective is that it can be used across a wide spectrum of team activities. At one end of the spectrum, AARs can be done by one or two people as a five-minute debrief on the spur of the moment. Or, at the other end of the spectrum, they can be used for a day-long off-site collaboration between several stakeholders of a large-scale project. Activities suitable for an AAR require a fixed beginning and endpoint, an identifiable purpose, and some basis for improvement in the future.

There are many versions of the AAR. But I think the version most suitable for improving a team's systems is based on three simple, but significant, questions:

- What systems, processes, and procedures are working well?
- What systems, processes, and procedures are not working well?
- What improvements or changes can we make for the future?

These three questions focus the mind of team members on appraising the positive and negative aspects of the systems in use in a project. As mentioned, AARs can be done casually or formally. Apart from gleaning gems of wisdom from the experiences of a project, the collaborative process of the AAR fosters a sense of commitment from participants to the outcomes of the review. Commitment comes from offering everyone an opportunity to participate and build consensus. Team members experience a sense of obligation to apply the key learnings.

The AAR is a useful tool for sharing the leadership—another characteristic of team identity. It provides all members of the team with a stake in the responsibility for team improvement.

Here are some examples of when an AAR can be used:

- when a new set of procedures or way of working has been introduced
- after a busy period when capacity was stretched
- following a trial period of a new system or procedure
- after a major training activity or
- between shifts.

This list isn't conclusive. The list does, however, provide you with a useful reference point.

The AAR is also useful for sharing tacit knowledge during the life of a project or activity. It provides a gateway to capture ideas from experienced team members and communicate with others. Legitimate short-cuts that are second nature to seasoned team members can be conveyed for the benefit of the whole team. Key learning points can be summarized before a team disbands, or before people forget what happened and move on to something else.

Despite the name ("after-action"), the review doesn't have to be performed at the end of a project or activity, as stated. An AAR can be performed after each identifiable milestone of a project or major activity. Doing a review at discernible phases means it becomes a method for live learning—lessons learned can be applied immediately.

Individuals can use an AAR for personal reflection. For instance, you can take a few minutes to reflect on something you did yesterday, such as attending a meeting with an important stakeholder, dealing with a complaint, or making an important telephone call. Ask yourself a variation of the three AAR questions mentioned earlier:

- What went well?
- What didn't go well?
- What can I do next time?

What do your reflections tell you about altering your approach next time?

Where the rubber meets the road

The Atlantic incident: Management response and the AAR

An AAR was conducted on March 15th at the State Forestry Offices in Dry Branch, Georgia. The Fish and Wildlife Service, Forest Service, Georgia State Forestry,

State Air Protection Branch, EPA, and media were all represented, in addition to members of the public and the prescribed burning community.

The atmosphere just prior to the AAR was tense. However, as the AAR commenced, the Forest Service began not by denying any blame for the incident but by apologizing for any inconvenience their burn had caused the public. That apology helped to make the participants from the air regulatory community much more willing to work together to describe and solve the problem in a cooperative manner.

While both prescribed burns were performed consistent with directions, it was clear that the existing tools for predicting, measuring, modeling, and managing prescribed burning at the regional level were insufficient. This is evidenced in the process of issuing burn permits at the time. While both the Piedmont and Oconee received permits from the same office, it is unclear whether the office was aware of the concurrent burns. The Georgia Forestry Commission issues burn permits from 130 offices throughout the State in the absence of coordination between the separate offices.

The AAR resulted in the following recommendations:

Establish certified smoke management program for Georgia.

Have the Georgia Forestry Commission manage permitting more regionally than locally.

Track permits real time for air quality management.

Communicate large acreage permits to the media.

Support accelerated USDA-Forest Service research for new smoke modeling.

Improve meteorology and modeling for regional air quality management of prescribed burning.

Assemble more data on the health impacts of such an intrusion on the metro area.

Gather data on local Atlanta emissions from fire impacts on such an intrusion.

Increase public education regarding prescribed burning especially for audiences in non-attainment areas.[59]

The systems a team uses can either be maintained, changed, or removed. Systems improvement isn't likely to occur unless there's a deliberate review process in place. In the busy life of a team, change won't happen without some planned attention. The AAR is a proven tool that can be used to examine a team's systems. Improving systems should become part of the culture of building a robust and responsive team.

In the next chapter, we consider the next characteristic of the high-performing team: utilizing diversity.

The top 10 key points

1. Systems feedback can be positive or negative, or a bit of both. Positive feedback on a system reinforces its current practice. Negative feedback suggests that corrective action is necessary to improve the system.

2. If systems aren't reviewed, there's little likelihood of their changing for the better.

3. Reviewing systems can be done in four ways.

4. Regular dialog is reviewing systems frequently and casually.

5. A check-in also means regular reviewing but doing so in a more structured and systematic way.

6. The end-of-project debrief is a flexible appraisal at the completion of a project.

7. The end-of-project report, as its name implies, is also carried out once a project has been finished, but done formally, either in a written or verbal format.

8. The AAR is a debriefing methodology that shares lessons from the past to make enhancements for the future.

9. The spirit of an AAR is based on openness and learning—it's not a tool for apportioning blame or finding fault.

10. The AAR was originally developed, and is still extensively used, by the US Army.

CHAPTER 19
Utilizing diversity

Appreciating the array of thinking styles needs to be considered when discussing the concept of diversity.

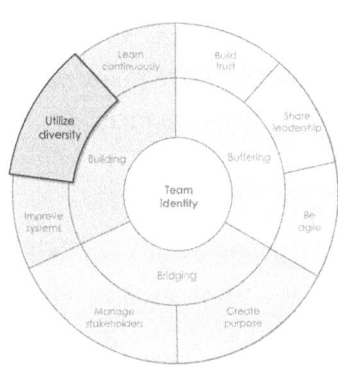

"**N**ew Zealand society has changed," says Graham Henry, former All Black coach. "It's not just Māori and European … the all Blacks team is made up of Tongan, Samoan, Fijian, Māori … and so the new haka encompasses the new culture and I think that is hugely important."

"We would stand up and talk about Fijian culture," he says, "and talk about Samoan culture … we might have a Samoan meal after that talk." It led to a "greater understanding of the guys you are playing with" and a better understanding of New Zealand society."[60]

We know that diversity matters. We also now know from research that diversity improves the bottom line of a business. Several recent studies we consider in this chapter show that companies in the top quartile for gender and ethnic diversity have financial returns above their national industry medians.[61] Simultaneously, firms lacking in diversity (in the bottom quartile) are not achieving above-average returns. These findings are transferrable to team success.

Diversity can offer a competitive advantage. Greater variety in a team's composition can be a competitive differentiator that shifts market share to more diverse companies over time.[62] A team—the main organizing structure of the modern workplace—that is diverse in its makeup can potentially lift its performance.

A cautionary note though: Correlation doesn't mean causation. Greater gender and ethnic diversity won't automatically translate into superior performance. A team actively committed to diversity shouldn't expect that this will guarantee better performance. There are many variables other than diversity that affect performance.

Indirect benefits of diversity

There's no doubting that diversity has indirect benefits—if not direct benefits—for team success. First, a more diverse workplace is better placed to attract top talent, for instance. A wider pool of quality applicants may be enticed to work in a team that's more reflective of the broader community. The reverse is true, too: A homogenous team may not be so appealing to standout applicants from an ethnic minority. Or, a team of older, more experienced members may not lure millennials to that working environment, despite the need for an injection of fresh ideas. Amongst other variables, sought-after talent in the marketplace may decide to apply for a job based on the diversity or a lack of diversity in a workplace.

Second, a team's capacity to communicate and engage externally can be influenced by its makeup. The ability to connect and participate with a wider audience can be boosted by the diversity of a team's membership. Generally, customers, stakeholders, and end-users are diverse, and matching this range of diversity can be a plus.

A third potential benefit of diversity is better shared decision-making. Managed well, a wider array of perspectives and viewpoints may lead to more considered solutions. This asset can only be tapped if the leader is committed to sharing leadership (see CHAPTER 9). Leaders comfortable in collaborating with colleagues can draw upon the collective wisdom of the team. With more opinions and perspectives, a better-informed decision may eventuate.

Conversely, a team that thinks alike—which is common—will have a thinner band of responses to a problem or dilemma. With similar perspectives, the less diverse team will effortlessly convince each other of the virtues of a solution, often stifling counter views. This is what's commonly referred to as *groupthink*[63]. As decision-making becomes more and more complex, a variety of perspectives—if available and encouraged—can be an asset.

In sum, there are ancillary benefits for attraction, engagement, and decision-making for diverse teams when that diversity is apparent and applied.

What about diversity in personality and thinking styles? Despite there being plenty of tools in the market to measure thinking styles and personality types, the way people think gets little attention in the diversity literature.

With no opportunity to proactively change team membership, leaders can still tap into people's thinking styles when the opportunity arises. Instead of getting irritated with people who don't think like us, we can use these different preferences to enrich the quality of team dialog and problem-solving. More about that later.

Diversity and performance

For now, consider the evidence of a link between diversity and performance. McKinsey has been examining diversity in the workplace for several years; researchers examined a range of industries in Canada, Latin America, the United Kingdom, and the US across 366 public companies. The research compared top management teams and their boards with financial metrics.[64]

What can we learn from McKinsey's findings? Companies in the top quartile for racial and ethnic diversity are 35 percent more likely to have financial returns above their respective national industry medians. Diversity starts at the team level, whether it's the executive or front-line teams, or in between. These findings suggest that recruitment and selection practices at the team level need to review their practices if they're not already doing so.

In terms of gender diversity, companies in the top quartile are 15 percent more likely to have financial returns above their respective national industry medians. Putting aside the argument for or against gender quotas, the research suggests a reasonable gender balance aids performance outcome.

At the opposite end of the scale, companies in the bottom quartile—both for gender and for ethnicity and race—are statistically less likely to achieve above-average financial returns. These findings reinforce the need for teams to consider diversity in its many forms.

In the US, this research shows a quantifiable connection between racial and ethnic diversity and better financial performance. For every 10 percent increase in racial and ethnic diversity on the senior executive team, earnings before interest and taxes (EBIT) rose 0.8 percent. Does this apply to non-executive teams?

Racial and ethnic diversity has a stronger impact on financial performance in the US than gender equity. The researchers speculate that this is because earlier efforts to increase women's representation in the top levels of business have already yielded positive results. Perhaps the message here is to strive where possible towards a reasonable gender balance as a starting point.

In the UK, gender balance on the senior executive team corresponded with highest performance. For example, for every 10 percent increase in gender diversity, EBIT rose by 3.5 percent. This reinforces the idea that diversity at the top end of the organization makes a difference and sets the tone throughout the business.

Interestingly, while certain industries perform better on gender diversity and others on ethnic and racial diversity, no industry or company in this study is in the top quartile on both dimensions. This suggests starting somewhere— anywhere—is important.

The authors conclude that diversity is a competitive differentiator. Diversity strategies can demonstratively shift market share. Viewing diversity as a competitive advantage is a sound strategy—apart from being the right thing to do—and supports utilizing diversity as a characteristic of winning teams. Diversity should be viewed both from a fairness perspective and as a driver of performance.

Other recent research, published in the *Harvard Business Review*, also reinforces the link between performance and diversity.[65] A survey of 1,700 companies across eight countries (the United States, France, Germany, China, Brazil, India, Switzerland, and Austria) and a variety of industries and company sizes, examines diversity in management positions. Diversity in this study considered gender, age, national origin, career path, industry background, and education levels.

The authors summarized their findings:

> We found that indeed there was a statistically significant relationship between diversity and innovation outcomes in all countries examined. Furthermore, the more dimensions of diversity were represented, the stronger the relationship was, although the precise patterns of diversity and performance were different across cultures. We also found that diversity had gained momentum as a topic in more than 70 percent of the enterprises surveyed, especially in developing economies.[66]

At the team level, the benefits of diversity—when harnessed—can be summarized in three ways:

- the capacity to make objective and accurate decisions
- enhanced analytical thinking by drawing upon a range of different perspectives and
- a willingness to try new approaches and be innovative.

These three benefits are additional to potentially better financial performance.

Where the rubber meets the road

Lessons learned in diversity

Stacy Brown-Philpot, the CEO of the freelance job site TaskRabbit, realized the importance of starting early when she reflected on her early days as a financial director at Google. "When I joined Google, it was 1,000 people," she said. "It took me two and a half years to look around and realize there weren't a lot of people like me. So [my colleague] David Drummond and I… put together a group. It was really late. I think that's part of the challenge [at Google]."

When Brown-Philpot moved to TaskRabbit, she took a different tack with the young company, partnering with the Congressional Black Caucus's CBC TECH 2020 initiative to bring more black workers into the tech industry. In 2016 Brown-Philpot publicly committed to increasing TaskRabbit's black workforce from 11 percent to 13 percent of employees by the year's end, to ensure proportional black representation at the company.[67]

Where to begin?

What can a leader do to improve diversity and inject fresh thinking into their team's deliberations? Here are some evidence-based suggestions that may help:[68]

Start early

Starting in the initial stages of team formation is the easiest option if it's possible. Once the team has developed, it's harder to address diversity. It's far easier to build a diverse team from scratch than to diversify a well-established team later. But if early intervention isn't an option, for well-established teams there are some other ideas to consider.

Small changes make big differences

Even one thoughtful change in a team's composition can make a significant difference to its outlook and approach. One new person with a nonconforming perspective can change a team's dynamic. If a new member of a team is prepared and encouraged to speak up and others are receptive to hearing a different perspective, they can challenge the team to consider alternatives.

However, there's a risk in inviting someone into a team who is distinct from the rest of the people in the team. The danger is that they may not be accepted by the others. The new team member may be ostracized or, at the very least, not listened to. But maintaining uniformity for the sake of harmony is a risk too. The risk is the team will not perform well. It's risky both ways. But the hazard of recruiting someone who's "different" into the team can be mitigated by the way it's managed.

Diversity beyond the team

Exposing a homogeneous team to alternative perspectives can broaden its horizon. Inviting speakers to team meetings to give another point of view can pay dividends, for example. I did this once when I combined a senior police team with the management team of an orchestra. Chalk and cheese, you might think. Surprisingly—to the participants at least—both teams came away realizing that they had more in common than not. This experience proved enlightening and reassuring for both teams.

Engaging mentors and coaches from diverse backgrounds can challenge team members to look at issues another way. If it's done sensitively and professionally, exposing team members to people who are less like them can be an enriching experience for both parties.

Calling out bias

A team leader, when they recognize it, should be courageous enough to tackle bias. If prejudice is overlooked and not challenged, it perpetuates its "legitimacy" in the eye of the holder of those views. What's more, when bias is denied or ignored, the perpetrator seeks out business partners, teammates, and employees who share their views. And in so doing, they further entrench their perspective and isolate themselves from differing outlooks that may be liberating.

People tend to react with anger and irritation when confronted about their biases—particularly when those prejudices are called out.[69] Although such interactions are awkward and sometimes unpleasant, they can lead to suitable change—these conversations can be an opportunity for growth. Bias isn't necessarily a permanent condition—but it can be, if not appropriately challenged.

Conditions for diversity

What are the enabling conditions for diversity? Fair employment practices, such as equal pay, participative leadership, top management support for diversity, and open communication channels, are some necessary factors. Yet less than 40 percent of companies adopt these fundamental conditions.[70] But firms with these factors in place are primed for better performance.

Having a diverse workplace doesn't, of course, guarantee higher performance. Promoting a harmonious work environment, devoid of hostility and with an inclusive culture, where different ideas are not just tolerated but genuinely sought and encouraged, is a sound basis.

One form of diversity I mentioned earlier in the chapter that's not spoken about in the literature is thinking styles. We've all clashed with or been confused by someone who thinks radically differently from us. Here are three typical illustrations of what I mean:

- People who prefer to think in the present and those who choose to think in the past or future.

- People who are energized by detail and others who are invigorated by the big picture.

- People who enjoy working with people and those who like working with things.

These differences in thinking preferences aren't as apparent as age and gender differences. Nonetheless, thinking style is a legitimate form of diversity and should be considered as such.

Human beings naturally harbor biases in the way they think. Detailed people become baffled with blue sky thinkers. Extroverts want introverts to speak up, and introverts want extroverts to shut up. People who are task-focused are not too interested in small talk, and relationship-focused people want to get to know the people they're going to work with first before executing the task. Diversity in the way people think and process the world can lead to irritation and prejudice—just as age, sex, and ethnicity can be confounding to some.

The array of thinking styles needs to be considered when discussing the concept of diversity. If thinking style is dismissed as a legitimate form of diversity, this can be just as damaging—sometimes more so—to relationships as any of the more obvious forms of prejudice. Awareness is key—just as it is for all forms of diversity.

In the next chapter, we further explore thinking styles as a valid form of diversity and how it can be channeled for team success.

The top 10 key points

1. Research suggests that diversity improves business performance.

2. Diversity can provide a competitive advantage.

3. Attraction, engagement, and decision-making are indirectly benefited by diversity and are all enablers of performance.

4. Diversity should be viewed both from a fairness perspective and as a driver of performance.

5. A causal relationship between diversity and performance is emerging.

6. It's far easier to build a diverse team from scratch than to diversify a well-established team later.

7. Even one thoughtful change to a team's composition can make a significant difference to its outlook and approach.

8. Exposing a homogeneous team to alternative perspectives can broaden its horizon.

9. A team leader, when they recognize it, should be courageous enough to tackle bias.

10. One form of diversity that's not spoken about in the literature is thinking styles.

CHAPTER 20

Harnessing work styles: the new form of diversity

Apart from conventional forms of diversity, such as gender and ethnicity, all teams harbor a variety of thinking styles—a less apparent form of diversity.

I n this chapter we explore thinking styles—another form of human diversity—and how the different ways people think can be utilized to improve team problem-solving capability. While there are myriad models available to identify the way people think, I'll refer to the *Margerison-McCann Team Management Wheel.* This model recognizes the preferences people have for work, based on the way they think, and what they offer their team beyond their functional capabilities. Apart from conventional forms of diversity, such as gender and ethnicity, all teams harbor a variety of thinking styles—a less apparent form of diversity.

Margerison and McCann's initial research into successful teams identified eight key types of work that contribute to effective problem-solving and performance.[71] This cycle of eight different work activities is a useful reference for considering thinking diversity and its impact on team effectiveness. The model has been applied in organizations around the world by drawing upon people's work preferences for problem-solving and boosting team effectiveness. These work activities are illustrated in a model known as the *Types of Work Wheel* illustrated in Figure 20.1 below.

Figure 20.1 Margerison-McCann Types of Work Wheel

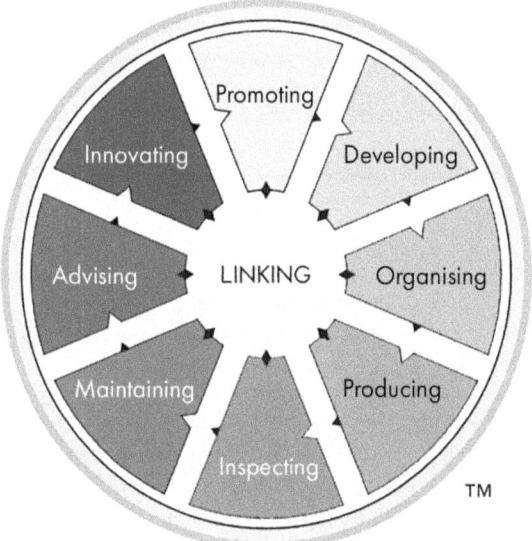

All eight work activities shown in the wheel apply to any complex problem-solving task. People have different preferences for how they like to involve themselves in group processes and problem-solving activities. Margerison and McCann investigated this further, aiming to identify a predictive relationship between who we are and what we like to do; that is, our thinking and work preferences.

These preferences constitute a significant influence on people's innate talents and applied strengths. Given the opportunity, team members will accentuate behaviors and work activities consistent with their thinking style. It follows that the more we can exercise that alignment of strengths in relevant work situations and team problem-solving, the more effective we become. This benefits the team member, their team, and the organization.

By combining data about individual work preferences with the Types of Work Wheel, the authors developed a model of team roles—the *Team Management Wheel*—which illustrates what we prefer to do and how we go about it. Figure 20.2 illustrates this model.

Figure 20.2 Margerison-McCann Team Management Wheel

Profiling employees using a psychometric feedback tool, the *Team Management Profile* (TMP) identifies people's preferences in the eight team roles above.

Based on their research, I'll briefly explain each of the eight types of work in their model, the behaviors that someone with preferences in each task may exhibit, and how a team member with that team role can apply their strength in the team environment. For more accurate and comprehensive feedback, an employee may complete a TMP.[72]

Advising

Advising work is concerned with gathering and giving information. It involves finding out what others are doing in their own area of work and ensuring that they are following best practice. Information may need to be gathered from articles, reports, or books, or by meeting and talking with people. It means ensuring that teams have all the information available for colleagues to make the best decision and deliver results.

People who are strong in Advising are referred to as *Reporter-Advisers*. Reporter-Advisers represent the classic advisory role in a team. They're talented at gathering information and packaging it in such a way that it can be readily understood by others. If they're more introverted, they'll tend to rely on a written format for their information, whereas if they're more extroverted, they're often empathetic communicators and probably rely on a network of colleagues and acquaintances for their data.

How can this strength of Advising be harnessed in a team? How this strength can be exercised is dependent on the person's current role in the team. For instance, in a business environment where the team member has some contact with customers or clients, Reporter-Advisors often have the inclination and aptitude to research customer attitudes towards the products and services the business provides. This information can then be compiled in a report or presentation at a team meeting. If a Reporter-Adviser is an internal service provider, they'll most likely be adept at investigating other organizational functions and how they may be dealing with similar issues: *What are they doing differently? What is the result? And can we use the same approach in our team?* These data can be reported back to the team. Reporter-Advisors will probably complete these assignments with relish and skill.

Innovating

As discussed through this book, *Innovating* is increasingly important in the modern workplace and involves challenging the way things are currently being done and coming up with new approaches. There is always a better way of doing things if people are prepared to consider alternatives.

People with preferences for Innovating tasks are referred to in the TMP as *Creator-Innovators*. Creator-Innovators are very much future-oriented and will enjoy thinking up new ideas and different ways of doing things. Usually, they're very independent and will pursue their ideas regardless of present systems and methods. They respond best when they are managed in such a way that their ideas can be developed without too many organizational constraints.

Applying the strengths of this role in the team allows people to challenge the status quo. Giving people with a preference for Innovating the scope and freedom to develop new, better, or different ways of tackling a problem is a good use of their talents. For instance, if the team member's job requires them to manage events, Creator-Innovators can be challenged to create a different and superior project planning system. The chances are they probably have already considered a new approach and may be waiting for their team leader to encourage them to put it into practice. Considering new approaches to existing problems plays to the strengths of the Creator-Innovator.

Promoting

To obtain the resources—people, money, and equipment—to carry out work, employees must sell what they're doing to key decision-makers. Resources to implement new ideas will only be given to a team if someone in that team can put a worthy case to persuade and influence people higher in the organization. Promoting to customers or clients both inside and outside the organization is also important to continually deliver what people want.

People who like to do the Promoting work are referred to as *Explorer-Promoters*. Explorer-Promoters can be excellent at taking ideas and advancing them to others, both inside and outside the organization. They enjoy being with people and will usually have a network of colleagues they use when gathering information and testing out opportunities. Explorer-Promoters are often advocating for change and are highly energized, active people with several different activities on the go at once. They enjoy being out and about and are good at bringing back contacts and resources that can help the team move forward.

In practical terms, this means that a team member with this approach will often excel in opportunities to liaise with stakeholders within and outside the organization. People with a talent for Promoting will most likely enjoy interacting with others professionally and socially. Inviting an Explorer-Promoter to present at a conference or business gathering will play to their strength. This is particularly the case if it involves an opportunity to sell a concept or product.

Developing

Many ideas don't see the light of day because they're impractical. The *Developing* task ensures that ideas are molded and shaped to meet the needs of customers, clients, or end-users. Developing involves listening to the needs of stakeholders and incorporating their responses into a workable plan.

People who prefer the task of Developing are referred to as *Assessor-Developers*. Assessor-Developers usually display a strong analytical approach to their work and are at their best when several different possibilities need to be analyzed and developed before implementation. They like coordinating new activities and respond well to such challenges, taking an idea and pushing it forward into a workable schema. Once the activity has been set up and proven to work, they'll tend to lose interest, preferring to move on to the next project rather than engage in the production and control of the output.

The application of this strength in the workplace is to think through how an idea can be adapted in the context of a team need. Assessor-Developers like to analyze and develop concepts to eventually be practical and operational. They're at their best when given an opportunity to implement a solution that works. The natural tendency of people with this strength is to think through the possible scenarios that could take place and how these situations may have an effect.

Organizing

Here the emphasis is on getting into action and making things happen. It involves *Organizing* the team so that everyone knows what they must do, how, and when. Clear project goals need to be established and action taken to ensure that results are delivered on time and to budget.

People who like Organizing are referred to by Margerison and McCann as *Thruster-Organizers*. Thruster-Organizers enjoy making things happen. They're analytical decision-makers, always doing what is best for the task, even if their actions sometimes upset others. They usually have a great ability to get things done, and for this reason, they're often found working in project management-type positions. People with this strength will *thrust* forward towards a goal, meeting conflict head-on if necessary. They emphasize targets, deadlines, and budgets, and will ensure that people are organized to act.

In practical terms, this means that a team member who is a Thruster-Organizer should be involved in organizing people and events. Being task-oriented, these people want outcomes—they get things done. Asking team members with this strength to coordinate projects, whether short-term or on-going, capitalizes on their talents. However, this doesn't mean they need to be the public face of the team or project group. They can be just as skillful behind the scenes. Either way, being task-oriented, they'll drive the project or event to an outcome. They may get impatient at team meetings and want to push the team to results. It's a good idea to capitalize on this and provide them with the opportunity to move to action if the discussion is meandering. The Thruster-Organiser will get people back on track and focused on the task at hand.

Producing

Once plans are set up and everyone knows what must be done, the team can concentrate on *Producing*. This activity focuses on delivering the product or service on a regular basis to high standards of effectiveness and efficiency. It's the Producing function that ensures the team keeps on delivering the required outputs consistently.

People who like to focus on the Producing work are referred to as *Concluder-Producers*. Concluder-Producers are practical and focus on the here and now; they can be counted on to carry things through to the end. Their strength is setting up plans and standard systems so that outputs can be achieved on a regular basis in a controlled and orderly fashion. For this reason, Concluder-Producers usually don't appreciate rapid change, as it interferes with the efficient systems they have established for doing the work.

Give team members with this preference tangible and practical tasks to accomplish. Concluder-Producers are concerned about the present—they may not be particularly interested in the past or future. They need and want to know what is required right here, right now. Bearing this in mind, Concluder-Producers will deliver on clear, tangible tasks that need to be done. Asking them to document the steps involved in a health and safety process will exercise this strength, for instance. Because of their practicality, they're searching for common-sense solutions. Therefore, asking Concluder-Producers what they think is the first step in a complex process is likely to precipitate a down-to-earth, practical answer. Concluder-Producers are usually looking for the next step and what needs doing.

Inspecting

Regular checks on work activities are essential to ensure that agreed standards are achieved. Quality audits of products or services will ensure that customers and end-users remain satisfied. *Inspecting* tasks also cover the financial aspects of work, as well as the security, safety, and legal aspects.

People with a preference for Inspecting are referred to as *Controller-Inspectors*. Controller-Inspectors are comfortable working within the rules and regulations established within and without the team. They would probably argue that the rules have been made to safeguard the team's working in the most resourceful manner and therefore everyone should obey them. For this reason, they enjoy working in situations where output is guided by organization or governmental regulations. They may work in finance, accounting, and quality-control positions, where their Inspecting preferences are important assets for the tasks they're doing.

In practical terms, this means that a team member with this preference is often skilled at developing benchmarks, KPIs, and processes for monitoring outcomes. They'll draw on past practices to add clarity for future processes. Asking a Controller-Inspector to create a new budget based on previous data will be an exercise that they'll likely feel comfortable doing. The historical data gives the Controller-Inspector tangible indicators to create a better future.

Maintaining

All teams need to uphold certain standards and maintain effective work processes to be effective. In the same way, your car will eventually break down if it doesn't have its regular service. Teams can fail, too, if the team processes and culture are not regularly checked and maintained. *Maintaining* ensures that values and quality standards are upheld and that regular reviews of team effectiveness take place to ensure sustainable performance.

People who like Maintaining activities are referred to in the TMP as *Upholder-Maintainers*. Upholder-Maintainers have strong personal values and beliefs which are of prime importance in their decision-making. Usually, they have a high concern for people and will be strongly supportive of those who share the same ideals and values they do. They prefer to work in a principle-oriented, supportive way, making sure that things are done according to their standards. In addition, they tend to prefer an advisory role in the background rather than a leading role. However, because of their strong principles, they may dig their heels in when confronting issues that oppose their beliefs.

The primary application of this team role is to monitor the sustainability and effectiveness of teamwork. Upholder-Maintainers will be very aware of potential fractures in the team or a team's not abiding by its own agreed standards. If encouraged to speak up, they can act as the team conscience.

Although these brief definitions are an overview, you can work with a TMP-accredited facilitator to access your own TMP online and get a deeper, more accurate idea of your strengths and talents, as well as the talents of others in your team.[73] By doing so, you're valuing and harnessing the diversity of thinking styles in the team.

As a team leader, you can utilize these preferences in decision-making and dialog across a variety of tasks and projects. At various times, key questions need to be considered to optimize a project or problem. Often, these questions are not addressed adequately, and performance can consequently suffer.

Here below is a summary of the eight questions critical to resolving most complex problems and the corresponding role preference best suited to raise and respond to the question.

Table 20.1 Eight key questions for complex projects

Key question	Type of work
What information do we need to resolve this problem?	Advising
What are some new ways to tackle the problem?	Innovating
Who do we need to support us to solve this problem?	Promoting
What would happen if we implemented this process this way?	Assessing
How can we organize the work to solve this problem?	Organizing
What are the key tasks that need doing?	Producing
How will we measure success?	Inspecting
How is the team collaborating to solve this problem?	Maintaining

This strategic problem-solving approach can draw upon the work preferences of team members, but only when those preferences are available, apparent, and appreciated. By sharing the leadership, the leader is exercising another form of diversity to lift performance—diversity in thinking styles.

In the next chapter, we will look at the final characteristic supporting the building function: learning continuously.

The top 10 key points

1. Margerison and McCann's initial research into successful teams identified eight key types of work that contribute to effective problem-solving and performance.

2. Reporter-Advisers represent the classic advisory role in a team.

3. Creator-Innovators are very much future-oriented and will enjoy thinking up new ideas and different ways of doing things.

4. Explorer-Promoters are excellent at taking ideas and advancing them to others, both inside and outside the organization.

5. Assessor-Developers usually display a strong analytical approach to their work and are at their best when several different possibilities need to be analyzed and developed before implementation.

6. Thruster-Organizers enjoy making things happen.

7. Concluder-Producers are practical and focus on the here and now; they can be counted on to carry

things through to the end.

8. Controller-Inspectors are comfortable working within the rules and regulations established within and without the team.

9. Upholder-Maintainers have strong personal values and beliefs which are of prime importance in their decision-making.

10. By sharing the leadership, the leader is exercising another form of diversity to lift performance— diversity in thinking styles.

CHAPTER 21
Learning continuously

Thinking outside the box is the new black.

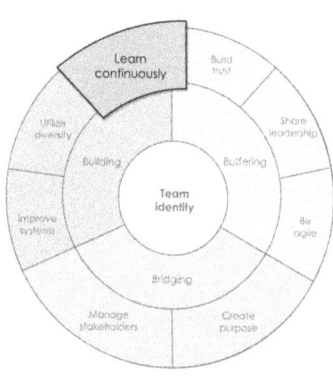

Marcia faces a dilemma. One of her five production teams is performing well below expectations. She ponders the array of learning and development options available to improve the team's performance. Is the poor performance the result of substandard technical knowledge? she wonders. Could the problem be non-technical, such as weak teamwork? Or, could the inferior performance be an inability to solve some of the challenging problems the team is bombarded with from their increasingly demanding customers? Questions to consider.

Marcia ponders whether lagging work performance could be resolved with personal rather than technical development. Perhaps the solution is learning some problem-solving skills to deal with the out-of-the-ordinary encounters the team faces from multiple stakeholders across and outside the company? The first step for Marcia is to investigate the matter further before acting.

After careful thought and further investigation, Marcia decides to apply three tactics to help the underperforming team improve its performance.

She plans to do a skills audit on each member of the team. Once this training needs analysis is done, Marcia plans to implement some technical training programs to boost the competency levels of each team member. She hopes a technical skills approach may lift team performance.

A second tactic Marcia considers is developing the non-technical capabilities of her team members. This approach will be based on personal growth, not technical skill development. Using this strategy, she decides to organize a team development workshop to build trust and better communication between team members. Marcia acknowledges that this team has had no exposure to communication training. Furthermore, this team was hastily put together, without any thought of how people would work (or not work) together. Yet she understands the extent to which team members rely upon each other to exchange information and share resources. The team's interactions are critical to getting the product out the door to the customer.

Marcia's third tactic is to adopt a problem-solving approach to build the team's decision-making capacity. To do this, a review of poor performance, including problem-solving and brainstorming meetings with—and between—members of the team, is to be undertaken. The complex nature of some of the problems facing this team means that under time pressure, wrong options are frequently taken. This alternative espouses lateral thinking to address some of the tricky challenges confronting the team in their day-to-day dealings with internal departments and stakeholders outside the business.

Each of the three approaches attacks the problem of poor performance from a different angle. One of these approaches—or a combination—is bound to work, Marcia thinks. She feels a renewed sense of confidence that the lagging performance issue can be overturned.

Tackling the problem from several perspectives offers her an array of possible solutions to solving the issue. Marcia concludes that by applying a multidimensional approach, she has more chance of being successful in resolving this challenging performance management problem.[74]

Learning continuously is the third characteristic supporting the bridging function of team identity. This chapter examines that characteristic.

The success of scientific management (discussed in CHAPTER 11) relies on teaching workers to comply with a one-and-only way of carrying out each job task. Effective learning this way is based exclusively on mastery of a series of prescribed job tasks. In the early days of scientific management, non-technical development programs were non-existent and considered unnecessary. Today, learning experiences that aren't job-specific are common—although not as common as technical training programs. Learning opportunities based on technical mastery of the job are still the norm.

Further, technical training is often viewed as the only real solution to performance improvement, even when the performance issue isn't necessarily job-specific. We need to break from the scientific management mindset and realize that technical training isn't the panacea for all performance improvements. An overreliance on job-centered training means that feasible non-technical learning options are often overlooked.

To perform in a turbulent marketplace requires more than technical skill. Technical mastery, of course, is still important. Job-specific training is aligned with the idea of specialization which still dominates the marketplace. Therefore, it is understandable why technical training is still the main dimension of learning in the workplace. I'm not disputing the relevance of strong technical competence. But to survive and prosper, individuals and teams need more than superior technical competence. Employees across all industries are facing a daily assault of unique and complex problems, challenges, and dilemmas that need resolving. Many of these predicaments can't be resolved by applying procedural knowledge learned from job skills training.

Thinking outside the box is the new black. There is rarely a neat, prescriptive answer to resolving knotty, left-field problems. The answer isn't always found in the company's procedure manual. With more and more out-of-the-blue challenges, people are required to think on their feet.

As we discussed in PART I, technical training doesn't teach people to think agilely. In practice, technical training does the opposite. This brand of learning requires the trainee to follow conventional pathways. Technical training assumes that work situations are predictable and by using an explicit approach, problems and challenges can be overcome.

Learning and development

There is a difference between *training* and *learning and development* (L & D). Training is a type of L & D—it's one of three dimensions. The primary focus of training is to develop the technical competence of the jobholder.

L & D covers both technical and non-technical development.

Consider the dilemma Marcia faced at the beginning of this chapter. She wisely chose a multidimensional L & D approach to overhaul a poorly performing team. Marcia's plan included technical and non-technical learning. It is wise to invest in both aspects to improve performance. By using both technical and non-technical learning options, a leader has more scope for development—they have more strings to their bow.

The non-technical approach of L & D covers two additional dimensions: personal development and problem-based learning. L & D is therefore made up of three dimensions of learning: training (technical) and personal development and problem-based learning (non-technical).

Learning continuously should adopt all three dimensions of L & D.

Where the rubber meets the road ...

Leaders are teachers

"We're always challenging the status quo," says legendary All Black coach and former schoolteacher, Graham Henry. "Always challenging the way we do things, both as an individual and as a team—how can we do things better? In fact, one of the pillars of the All Blacks environment is that it is devoted to learning; the management of students of the game, constantly looking for the edge."[75]

Based on the three dimensions of L & D, the focus is either job-related, person-related, or problem-related. These three dimensions are the pillars of learning continuously. We explore the job- and person-related dimensions in this chapter and problem-related learning in the next chapter.

Of the three dimensions, the job-related component has been the more popular dimension for the past 100 years, since the birth of scientific management. With the transformation of work and the shift from local to global marketplace, the job-related dimension is inadequate on its own to enhance performance.

Performing in the workplace is now more than job mastery. Non-job behaviors such as being adaptable and showing enterprise, for example, are attributes of high performers in the 21st century (see CHAPTER 12). These personal qualities (non-technical) can, and should be, developed, but technical training programs don't effectively teach people to be adaptable and enterprising. Therefore, individuals and teams now require a multidimensional approach that embraces all three dimensions of L & D.

The learning approach a manager chooses to solve performance problems says something about their beliefs about the role of employees. If a manager views an employee as a commodity, that is, as a cog in the wheel of production, they will likely favor the job-related approach. In contrast, a leader who sees team members as partners will be more open to person-related learning. A leader's attitude to learning is often shaped by their expectations of the people who work for them.

So, in summary, I have categorized the three dimensions of L & D:

- job-centered
- person-centered and
- problem-centered

Each dimension has a clear emphasis.

Let's take a closer look at the job- and person-centered dimensions.

Job-centered

The conventional learning approach in the workplace is still job-centered. I would guess that approximately 80 percent of learning activities in organizations could be classified as job-centered.

This dimension emphasizes job skills training. The popularity of job-centered training is due to the obvious connection between job skills development and job performance. Developing the skills of a jobholder to directly improve their job performance is the primary reason for investing in job-centered training. Of the three dimensions, the job-centered approach is the one directly associated with job performance.

Training programs that improve a person's capacity to operate a piece of machinery, to master some form of technology, or to learn a work-related system or process, for example, are job-centered. These activities are tasks a jobholder is required to complete as part of their job.

Learning anything straight from a jobholder's job description can potentially lead to better on-the-job performance. Quality job-specific training, in other words, directly boosts an employee's job performance. The aim of job-centered training is to produce a more technically proficient jobholder. For this reason, it is understandable why most organizations devote much of their L & D budget to job-centered training programs.

Apart from benefitting the employer, job-centered training programs can benefit the jobholder directly and indirectly. Being more technically proficient makes the jobholders' job easier and less stressful. Technical training, in other words, helps a team member to perform their job with more confidence and greater proficiency. Better job performance may lead to promotion and more pay. For these reasons, this dimension of L & D is attractive to the employee too.

Unsurprisingly, the job-centered approach—appealing to both employer and employee—has many advocates who argue passionately for its merits and application in the workplace.[76] The job-centered dimension is designed to induce employee conformity to the sponsoring organization's needs.

Born from the scientific management movement, job-centered training positions the employee as an anonymous agent of the organization. The employee surrenders their individuality to fit into the production aims of the employer. With no real scope for original thought and autonomy, the jobholder is expected to passively comply with the constraints of the organization. Although the employee acquires job skills that can benefit them and possibly their career, the job-centered dimension of L & D is primarily focused on the interests of the employer.

Person-centered

The person-centered dimension emphasizes self-development—it involves an investment in the personal rather than the technical growth of the employee. While job-centered training has an explicit link to the job description, the person-centered approach has an implicit connection to job performance.

The motive for an organization to sponsor person-centered development is the same as the job-centered approach, that is, to enhance job performance. But it is a different orientation. With the person-centered approach, the learning experience aims to develop the person. Performance is derived from personal development rather than technical development.

Unlike the job-centered dimension, person-centered learning can circuitously—rather than directly—increase productivity. The assumption supporting a person-centered approach is that a more developed person becomes a more accomplished jobholder either immediately or in the future. Training programs that improve a person's self-mastery include subjects like goal setting, personal motivation, time management, and emotional intelligence. These personal capabilities augment job performance.

The incentive for leaders to sponsor self-development opportunities is that when people's personal capabilities are built up, they become more capable team members. Further, person-centered learning is based on the belief that through personal growth, people—the organization's most precious resource—will be more successful in their work role. Over the last 30 years, the proliferation of personal development experiences, courses, and activities suggests this premise is well-founded.

Both the person- and job-centered dimensions benefit the individual and organization. While benefiting job performance incidentally, personal development extends a jobholder's capabilities beyond their technical skill set. The prospects to develop, improve, and enrich an employee's personal and technical capabilities is appealing to employee and employer.

Of the two L & D dimensions, however, the person-centered method—despite its growing popularity—is the less attractive for employers. With the weaker connection between personal development and job performance, investing in person-centered learning is the less favored learning option in most cases. Job-centered training, on the other hand, promises immediate application to improving job performance.

Despite this distinction, job- and person-centered learning have two things in common, apart from developing the employee. The two similarities relate to their rationale and application. First, both types of learning are undertaken principally to advance the interests of the sponsoring organization. Although the employee benefits in both cases, their needs are subordinate to those of the employer. The rationale for both approaches is to get better productivity in the employee's current role.

Second, both approaches to learning are typically formulaic. Participants have little scope for exercising independent thinking. For instance, it's conventional practice for a participant attending a personal development training program to faithfully follow the direction of the trainer. What's more, the course content is usually predetermined. The trainer follows a set training curriculum. Notwithstanding the specific needs of attendees to these personal development programs, they are given little option but to abide by the content of the prearranged program.

Despite the rhetoric of *self-discovery*, there's no real opportunity to engage in any autonomous expression in most personal development programs. The trainee merely reacts to the trainer's instructions and follows the sequence of activities laid out in the training manual.

Person-centered development courses are usually based on a *how to* formula or a step-by-step process, like technical training programs.

To illustrate my point, consider, for example, a *Five Steps to Better Listening* communication program. The trainer typically leads workshop participants sequentially through the five steps during the program, regardless of its relevance to their current needs. Undoubtedly, these programs have merit and can be informative and fun. Moreover, procedural knowledge is valuable and necessary for learning many skills. But too much attention on routine training can undercut the individual's capacity for real personal growth. In short, person-centered training delivered in a formulaic way does undermine the fundamental and inherent self-determination of the individual.

Despite the organization-centric motive for job- and person-centered training and its adherence to a set format, these L & D programs do play an important role in elevating individual and organizational success.

In the next chapter, we consider the third dimension of L & D: the problem-centered approach and the application of a multidimensional approach needed for continuous learning.

The top 10 key points

1. The success of scientific management relies on teaching workers to comply with the one-and-only way of carrying out each job task.

2. To perform in a turbulent marketplace requires more than technical skill.

3. Technical training doesn't teach people to think agilely.

4. Training is a type of learning and development—it's one of three dimensions.

5. L & D is multidimensional.

6. Learning continuously is the third characteristic supporting the bridging function of team identity.

7. The three dimensions of L & D are job-centered, person-centered, and problem-centered.

8. The job-centered dimension covers technical job mastery.

9. The person-centered dimension emphasizes self-development.

10. The problem-centered dimension focuses on learning from a problem.

CHAPTER 22

Applying the multidimensional learning model

Learning continuously is more than frequently sending people off on public training programs.

Julie—executive manager of L & D for a large bank— was charged with the responsibility of revamping the bank's approach to inducting customer service representatives (CSRs) in retail banking services. After looking at the high turnover rates and gathering information from a series of conversations she had with CSRs and their managers, she decided it was time to act.

From what Julie heard in these conversations, the bank had a challenge in reducing the high rates of turnover in the first 12 weeks of their employment with the bank. Employees had told her that they didn't have enough product knowledge and enough confidence interacting with customers. Changing the induction program's learning methods was the place to start, Julie concluded.

The induction training was too prescriptive and procedural and didn't factor in many of the real issues and problems CSRs faced on the job.

Julie's new induction program enables new CSRs to

analyze situations and source information more effectively. The program is supported by continuous coaching, involving partnering between participants, their branch manager, and a "buddy" who's an experienced CSR. With this additional support, new recruits are expected to take ownership of their learning and complete a series of practical tasks to better prepare them for their new role. CSRs work with their branch manager to identify their strengths and areas of improvement through daily check-ins, debriefs, and feedback sessions.

Collaborative coaching, problem-based learning, simulations, and research are now part of the induction training. During the initial off-the-job learning period, participants work in groups and explore customer situations that they'll likely encounter. Using simulations, CSRs are encouraged to examine a scenario and explore how they would respond to complete customer transactions. In the first six months of its inception, the revamped CSR induction program has delivered an eight percent reduction in voluntary turnover.[77]

In the last chapter, I explained the dimensions of the multidimensional learning model. These three dimensions are job-, person-, and problem-centered learning. Each dimension is integral to learning continuously—the eighth and final characteristic of the Team Identity model. I defined the job- and person-centered approaches in the previous chapter. Now we take a closer look at the problem-centered approach—the third dimension in the model.

Learning continuously should embrace all three dimensions of learning. By using the multidimensional learning model, a leader has a wide array of possible solutions to optimize performance. We'll discuss the application of the model later in the chapter.

Where the rubber meets the road

Skills before muscle

New Zealand focuses on skills development at age-group level rather than muscle; strength and conditioning come later. By focusing on skills during the formative years of players, when they are at their most impressionable, rather than gym sessions, the All Blacks can think their way out of trouble. Of course, strength, stamina, and power are requisite components of a competitive side at the top level, but too many teams are strong in the elements that can easily be coached and lacking in those that rely on something ingrained in players. The emphasis is multidimensional.[78]

Let's define the third dimension of L & D before considering the model.

Problem-centered

As the name implies, the problem-centered approach is about problem-solving, that is, learning to be more capable at dealing with out-of-the-blue work-related challenges. The focus of this approach is to develop the capacity to analyze and resolve problems at work. With improved problem-solving capability, people can make better decisions on the job.

The motivation for problem-centered learning is the connection between solving problems and improved performance. Investing in problem-centered learning is justified by the escalating and unpredictable challenges employees now face. In their day-to-day work, people can make better informed decisions to deal with random problems, increasing challenges, and difficult dilemmas. Development of one's decision-making aptitude therefore makes sense.

With greater problem-solving capability, employees can exercise more freedom and autonomy in their work. They are less likely to rely on their leader to make decisions they can make themselves. With more skill and confidence in dealing with ambiguous issues affecting their work, people are more independent to exercise their judgment in solving challenging problems.

And the more confident and self-sufficient a person becomes, the less the strain they put on their leader. The team member becomes more self-assured and independent. What's more, having a reputation as a good problem-solver enhances their employability.

You'll recall that *autonomy* was cited as one of three intrinsic motivational forces we discussed in CHAPTER 9. The capable team member—one who can solve a wider array of work problems—has more freedom and greater self-confidence to make decisions and choices. Greater self-sufficiency is also motivating.

Subjects such as creative problem-solving techniques, research skills, and analyzing real-world cases are examples of problem-centered learning. Problem-based learning is a blend of thinking and acting differently to tackle tricky problems. Examining critical incidents and real-life scenarios can serve as a springboard for better decision-making in the future. By contemplating these situations in constructive ways, teams build knowledge, develop understanding, and can agree upon a better way when similar dilemmas arise.

The After-action Review we discussed in CHAPTER 18 is an effective form of problem-centered learning. Based on the three questions *What went well? What didn't go so well?* and *What will we do differently next time?* the AAR is an effective debriefing tool. Although it can be used for multiple purposes, the AAR can be used as a process for continuous improvement.

With these obvious benefits, it remains a mystery why problem-based learning isn't used more frequently in the workplace. Learning from a problem typically happens only after a crisis, when the team has no option other than preventing the incident from repeating itself in the future. Problem-centered learning should occur in positive circumstances too. People are generally upbeat and less inclined to be defensive after a successful campaign or project—they will undoubtedly be in a receptive frame of mind to learn in these constructive circumstances.

Considering the relevance of problem-solving today, why isn't there more emphasis on this type of learning? After all, when applied properly, this dimension of learning inevitably leads to quality decisions. With a focus on real-life problems and situations, the problem-centered approach is the most practical form of learning of the three dimensions.

Furthermore, problem-centered learning improves agility. *Problem-solving* is one of the seven dimensions of the Team Agility model we covered in CHAPTER 11. Problem-solving positively impacts on *customer responsiveness*, another dimension of agility. Being agile and learning continuously work in tandem.

Although slow to take hold—even with its obvious benefits—problem-centered learning is gradually gaining prominence across industries and cultures. The more complex and less predictable working environment we now face is undoubtedly the catalyst for the steady take-up of problem-based learning.

Problem-centered learning should be considered in concert with the other two dimensions of learning. The ability to think laterally, creatively, and flexibly is no longer discretionary. Intense global competition puts mounting pressure on businesses to treat every customer request promptly and competently to stay viable. Doing so means abandoning stock standard problem-solving templates. Fickle customers, demanding end-users, and essential stakeholders are less and less tolerant of being "processed."

Being able to take an exceptional circumstance and deal with it confidently and capably is a skill set everyone benefits from, including team members, customers, and company. The longstanding myth that the technically superior team is the gold-plated pathway to high performance overrates job-centered training and undervalues person- and problem-centered learning. All three dimensions have their place in high performance.

Even though personal development and problem-based learning are indispensable in a VUCA environment, they still account for only a minority of L & D expenditure. With 80 percent of expenditure on job-centered training and 20 percent allocated to the other two dimensions, organizations are slow to fully embrace a multidimensional approach where all three approaches are equally valid.

Being an agile problem-solver depends largely on non-technical attributes. These are the non-job roles we discussed in CHAPTER 12. Given the increasing relevance of non-job roles, personal- and problem-centered learning approaches are more applicable now. Teams need to shift from a job-centered emphasis to the multidimensional L & D strategy.

Multidimensional learning model

There are strong advocates with compelling arguments for the value of each dimension of learning. All three have their place; they are all valid. Each dimension has a role to play in individual and team development. Instead of arguing which approach is superior, applying them all takes advantage of the strengths of each dimension. A multidimensional approach to learning strategy brings to light the value of each perspective.

The question underpinning the multidimensional learning model is *What does each L & D dimension have to offer in strengthening individual and team performance?* Applying the multidimensional learning model helps the team in more than one way.

Where the rubber meets the road

Lagging work performance in Zac's team

Zac is a leader facing the challenge of overturning lagging work performance in his team. He can respond to substandard performance in one of three ways or apply the multidimensional learning model. The performance issue could be tackled from a personal efficiency

---

perspective. Using the person-centered approach, the answer might be to improve the way Zac's team manages its workload. Specifically, this means training his team members to manage themselves and their priorities more adeptly. By contemplating a time management program, Zac would deal with the performance issue through personal development.

Looking at the problem from another angle, Zac could consider that poor technical competence is the root cause of poor performance. So, a job-centered approach might be the best way forward to remedy any technical deficiencies within the team. Zac may decide that his team should undertake a competency-based training program in *Excel*—a program his team uses regularly in its work. Advancing team members' technical skill may lift their performance.

A third option open to Zac is to apply the problem-centered approach. Consistent with this method, he considers facilitating a workshop to discuss some of the key problems his team has encountered over the past three months. The purpose of the workshop is to identify some ways of dealing with these problems, drawing upon the collective wisdom of the team.

Any one of these three approaches, or a combination, will probably provide Zac with the solution to the dilemma of his poor team performance.

A leader choosing more than one dimension of L & D broadens their options. And by adopting a multidimensional model of learning, the leader's odds for resolving performance matters are boosted.

To promote the characteristic of learning continuously, I'd recommend approximately one-third of the team's learning budget be allocated to each of the three dimensions. This extends the array of L & D options and fosters a more eclectic learning culture within the team.

In practice, a balanced L & D budget translates to a third of expenditure on the self-development of team members (person-centered approach), a third for specific training to carry out job skills (job-centered approach), and a third towards building problem-solving capacity (problem-centered approach). This mix reinforces the legitimacy of L & D as an enabler of higher performance, balances the needs of the individual and organization, and offers leaders more options. Learning continuously is more than frequently sending people off on public training programs. Each of the three dimensions has its merits and place in the high-performing team's L & D program.

This brings us to the end of PART II. We've traversed eight characteristics of winning teams. These eight characteristics are the important ingredients in shaping a strong team identity. They reinforce the three overarching functions of team identity: buffering, bridging, and building.

In summary, building trust, sharing leadership, and being agile support buffering. Buffering is protecting the team from disruptive outside forces that waylay a team's progress. The characteristics of creating purpose and managing stakeholders strengthen bridging. Bridging is reaching out to key alliances that can assist—or if neglected, hinder—a team's progress. Improving systems, utilizing diversity, and learning continuously support building. Building is the process of developing a robust team culture.

In PART III, I provide you with a process for measuring and monitoring the health of your team's identity. Through this analysis, you can identify the team's strengths and opportunities for growth. This information assists you to create a plan of action for increasing performance that emphasizes the people dimension of teamwork.

The top 10 key points

1. The problem-centered approach is about problem-solving, that is, learning to be more capable at dealing with out-of-the-blue work-related challenges.

2. The motivation for problem-centered learning is the connection between solving problems and improving performance.

3. People can make better informed decisions to deal with random problems, ambiguous challenges, and difficult dilemmas in their day-to-day work.

4. Subjects such as creative problem-solving techniques, research skills, and analyzing real-world cases are examples of problem-centered learning.

5. With greater problem-solving capability, employees can exercise more freedom and autonomy in their work.

6. Having a reputation as a good problem-solver enhances a person's employability.

7. The longstanding myth that the technically superior team is the gold-plated pathway to high performance overrates job-centered training and undervalues person- and problem-centered learning.

8. To promote the characteristic of learning continuously, I'd recommend approximately one-third of the team's learning budget be allocated to each of the three dimensions.

9. In practice, a balanced L & D budget translates to a third of expenditure on the self-development of team members (person-centered approach), a third for specific training to carry out job skills (job-centered approach), and a third towards building problem-solving capacity (problem-centered approach).

10. Each of the three dimensions has its merits and place in the high-performing team's L & D program.

PART III

How to measure team identity

CHAPTER 23

Team profile and action-plan

The dilemma in any change initiative is knowing where to begin.

In this final chapter, I will provide you with a practical step-by-step action-planning process to strengthen the people dimension of your team. This process is based on the Team Identity model and the eight characteristics discussed in PART II. Often the dilemma in any change initiative is knowing where to begin; it's no different for enhancing team performance: *Where do I start?*

I suggest the place to commence is to establish some clear benchmarks, based on the Team Identity model. These benchmarks will answer two important questions:

- How is your team traveling against the eight characteristics of high performance?
- What are the teams' strengths and opportunities for growth?

By benchmarking the team against each characteristic, you can then develop an action plan to boost performance. With clarity on where to begin the process of development, you can focus your time and energy. The focus can then be applied to one characteristic in the model. Even though you are concentrating your attention on one characteristic, progress will most likely impact other characteristics.

Should you require more support beyond these final pages, you are welcome to contact me.[79]

Here below is an illustration in Figure 23.1 of the steps in the action plan.

Figure 23.1 Action plan

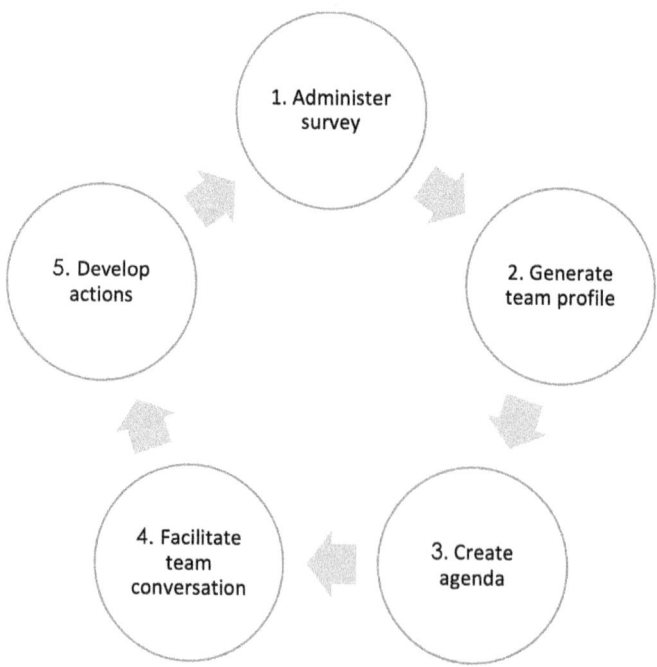

The first thing you'll probably notice about the action plan is that it's cyclical rather than linear. Action planning in this case is an on-going process that becomes part of team development each year from now on.

I'll now walk you through each of the five steps.

1. Administer survey

The first task is to establish who you want feedback from to give you a realistic picture of how the team is performing. In the survey, there are three perspectives to consider:

- team leader
- team members and
- stakeholders (internal and external).

With three perspectives, the survey is what's commonly referred to as a "360" or multi-rater approach. Multiple perspectives consider the views of those who are part of the team and those who deal with the team. Using a multi-rater approach, a comparison is made between the perspectives of the team leader, team members, and stakeholders. This method is more comprehensive than just surveying one perspective, such as team members.

Selecting the first two inputs (team leader and team members) is straightforward. Choosing stakeholders for their input, however, requires some thought. Ideally, you want a blend of internal and external stakeholders. Internal stakeholders are defined as people outside the team but within the organization the team is part of. For example, internal stakeholders may include the team leader's boss and others whom the team interacts with frequently inside the organization. I would aim for three or more internal stakeholders who can make informed judgments about the team.

External stakeholders are people outside the organization who are qualified to comment on the team's conduct. Like internal stakeholders, these externals must have regular contact with the team. They can be customers, suppliers, or end-users. Regardless of their relationship with the team, these stakeholders need to be able to evaluate the team on matters such as trust within the team, leadership style, and approaches to learning. If possible, aim for two or three external inputs.

If your team doesn't deal with the public, then you can just select five or more internal stakeholders. Nonetheless, with three perspectives—team leader, team members, and stakeholders, the survey data provides a wide-ranging 360-degree view of the team.

The team profile is administered online, so you'll need permission from all team members and stakeholders selected to participate in the survey. On gaining their approval, all participants are sent an invitation online to complete the survey. The survey should take no more than 15 minutes to complete. Each participant is issued with a unique key to protect their anonymity. This means individual responses can't be attributable to anyone. The team leader—being a one-person perspective—is the only person whose anonymity isn't protected.

2. Generate team profile

Once participants have completed the survey, a team's profile report is generated. The report covers 80 statements (10 for each characteristic). Although randomized in the survey, the statements and their responses in the report are organized into eight sections. Furthermore, the characteristics are grouped under the three functions of team identity we covered in PART I: buffering, bridging, and building.

For each characteristic, the 10 statements are crafted

around KPIs covered in PART II. Below is the team profile structure and a summary of the relevant KPIs.

Buffering

- Building trust (evidence of leading by example, open communication channels, and robust working relationships within the team).

- Sharing leadership (evidence of appropriate democratic decision-making, a climate of enterprise and initiative, suitable freedom and autonomy to make decisions, and a willingness by the leader to adopt a coaching leadership style).

- Being agile (evidence of innovation and continuous improvement, a commitment to speedy processing, quick recovery from mistakes, and responsiveness to stakeholders).

Bridging

- Creating purpose (evidence of a clear team purpose, a commitment to that purpose, and a willingness to communicate purpose beyond the team).

- Managing stakeholders (evidence of setting and managing expectations, ability to engage and work with stakeholders, and readiness to understand the needs of stakeholders).

Building

- Improving systems (evidence of creating opportunities to examine the team's systems, holding regular improvement discussions and debriefs, involving all team members in systems improvement, and reviewing and assessing new approaches to getting the work done).

- Utilizing diversity (evidence of exposing the team to new perspectives, tackling bias, and using different thinking styles).

- Learning continuously (evidence of an on-going commitment to learning and a balanced learning agenda of job-, person-, and problem-centered approaches).

You can contact me for more information on the survey content.[80]

Participants answering the survey statements have three options: *agree, disagree,* or neither agree nor disagree (*neither*). A "neither" response can be posted for several reasons. "Neither" could be an indication that an observable behavior is sometimes consistent with the statement and at other times it's not apparent; in other words, the behavior is inconsistent. Or, it could mean that the respondent doesn't know or isn't entirely convinced to "agree" or "disagree" with a statement. It could also mean there is scope for improvement.

Let's turn to one of the two graphics in the team profile report. The first graphic—summarizing each characteristic—illustrates the extent of agreement and disagreement (congruence) for the 10 statements related to that characteristic. The other graphic is a straightforward histogram showing the percentage of aggregate agreement and disagreement responses for the three perspectives. I'll elaborate on the first of these two graphical representations.

The figure below illustrates the seven possible outcomes for a response to a statement.

Figure 22.2 Potential outcomes for each characteristic

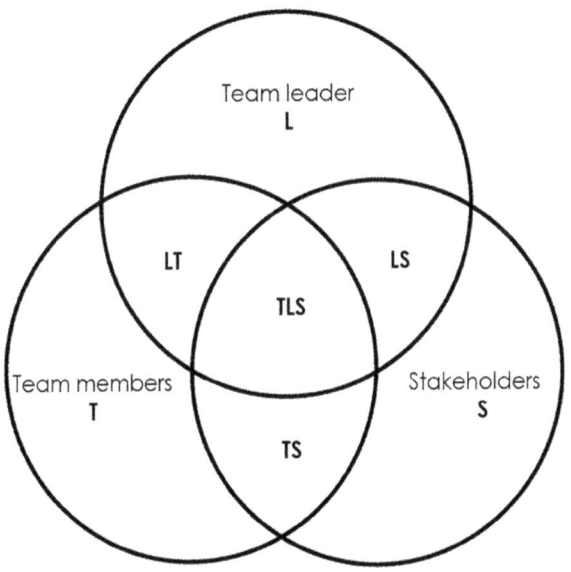

- **T** represents an aggregate view shared exclusively by Team members.

- **L** represents an aggregate view shared exclusively by the Team leader.

- **S** represents an aggregate view shared exclusively by Stakeholders.

- **LT** represents an aggregate view shared by Team members and the Team leader, but not Stakeholders.

- **LS** represents an aggregate view shared by the Team leader and Stakeholders, but not Team members.

- **TS** represents an aggregate view shared by

Team members and Stakeholders, but not the Team leader.

- **TLS** represents an aggregate view shared by all three perspectives.

The aggregate result, wherever it arises in the graphs in the team profile report, can be positive; that is, there's a majority view in one, two, or three perspectives that agreed with a statement. Further, this suggests a general perception that a KPI is evident. Or, the opposite might be the case; that is, one or more of the three perspectives disagreed with a statement. This suggests an overall perception that a KPI is not apparent. An aggregate positive or negative result shared by all three perspectives (represented in the **TLS** space in the graphic) would indicate there's overwhelming or underwhelming agreement or disagreement respectively for a statement. Results in the **TLS** space can suggest a strength (positive result) or opportunity for growth (negative result) in the team profile.

The third possible response is a mixed or "polarized" response. These results indicate varied opinions about a statement, without a majority favoring any particular outcome. A polarized response can occur in all areas except **L**. Since **L** represents the exclusive view of one person—the team leader—only three results are possible: "agree," "disagree," or "neither agree nor disagree." But in the other six areas on the graphic, where there is more than one input, a polarized result is possible. Polarized means there is an even split between "agree" and "disagree" responses for a statement in the survey.

A polarized result could show up in the Team (**T**) or Stakeholder (**S**) perspectives or between two perspectives

(**LT, TS,** or **LS**). If the view within one or two perspectives is polarized, it's signified by the figure "0." Polarized responses, wherever they show up in the profile, can be interpreted in several ways and need to be discussed with the team to understand their possible meaning.

The final type of result is "neither." A "neither" response to a statement can be illustrated in the profile in one or more of the three perspectives (**T, S,** and **L**). This occurs when the aggregate response for Team members, the Team leader, or Stakeholders is "neither" for a statement.

All seven possible aggregate results (**T, S, L, LT, LS, TS,** and **TLS**) can be significant. To illustrate, an aggregate "agree" or "disagree" result shared by all three perspectives (represented in **TLS** in Figure 2.2) suggests an overwhelming perception that a KPI is either observable or imperceptible in the team. For example, consider an aggregate "agree" result (represented as **TLS**) for the following two survey statements:

- The Team leader leads by example most of the time.

- He/she walks the talk.

Where all three perspectives (including that of the Team leader) "agree" with these two statements, this indicates a strong perception that the team leader does lead by example (a KPI for building trust). On the other hand, an aggregate "disagree" result (again in **TLS**) for both statements would point to an overwhelming opinion (including that of the Team leader) that the leader does not lead by example. Whilst results recorded in **TLS** are definitive, other results recorded in the intersections between the three perspectives (**LT, TS,** & **LS**) are less so.

By discussing the results of the profile report with the team, a better understanding of the range of perceptions can be determined. Questions such as:

- Why were the Team and Stakeholders positive about this KPI, even though the Team leader was not?

- What have others observed that the Team leader hasn't?

can be put by the leader to the team.

Asking these types of questions may clarify the profile's results and builds greater understanding.

The team profile report is a catalyst for a team conversation. Results in the report don't explain the reasons for similar or differing perceptions between and within the three perspectives. However, the report does provide a sound basis for developing an agenda for a constructive team discussion. More about the team conversation shortly.

Figure 23.3 below provides a real-life team example of the summary outcome for the characteristic of being agile.

Figure 23.3 Being agile

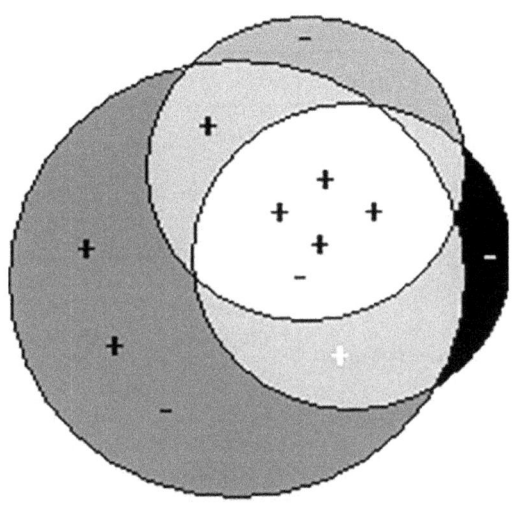

Team	
Team leader	
Stakeholders	

In the example above, a "+" symbol represents an aggregate positive result. Aggregate negative results are shown as a "-" symbol.

Note the Team members and Stakeholders circles are smaller than the Team leader circle. Each time an aggregate response to a statement is "neither," the radius of the circle reduces by 10 percent. The smaller a circle, the more aggregate "neither" responses from the participants representing that perspective.

Data in the report is represented statistically too. Table 23.1 on the next page shows an illustration of one statement from a team profile.

Table 23. 1 Statistical representation

Q.4 The team has built constructive working relationships with its key stakeholders.		
Team leader	Agree	
Team	Agree	• agree: 75% (6/8) • neither: 12.5% (1/8) • disagree: 12.5% (1/8)
Stakeholders	Disagree	Internal • agree: 33.3% (2/6) • neither: 33.3% (2/6) • disagree: 33.3% (2/6) External • agree: 20% (1/5) • neither: 20% (1/5) • disagree: 60% (3/5)

Each of the 80 statements is represented statistically, like the one above. Survey participants can also make comments that are reflected in the report in a different section.

In summary, the team profile report is formatted into the three functions of team identity. Within each function, data for the supporting characteristics are presented. Each characteristic is represented in summary as in Figure 23.3 and in histogram format. Below these two graphics are the statistical results of the 10 statements related to that characteristic, like Table 23.1. And at the end of the report are anonymous comments from participants.

3. Create agenda

The next step in the action planning process is selecting one characteristic from the profile for a team discussion. The purpose here is to use the survey data to guide and inform a team conversation. Select the characteristic with the most potential for improvement. Developing one characteristic will permeate other characteristics. Improving one aspect of the people dimension of teamwork—with interdependencies between characteristics—is likely to positively affect other areas.

Instead of being paralyzed with myriad options, focusing on one characteristic at a time is a sound strategy. So, the agenda for discussion should be confined to one characteristic in the profile report.

4. Facilitate team conversation

To assist you to facilitate a constructive team conversation, here are some good questions to start the team discussion:

- Do the results for this characteristic surprise you or not? Why? How?
- What are some examples to verify these findings?
- What can we do as a team to improve this characteristic?
- How will we go about this?

5. Develop actions

From the team discussion, the next step is to develop some practical and realistic actions. Use the tools and practical suggestions in PART II. For example, if managing stakeholders is an opportunity for improvement, then use the SPIR model from CHAPTER 16 as the tool for improving your team's stakeholder relationships.

To monitor team progress, repeat the cycle, beginning with another team profile report. I recommend completing the survey annually. Steps 3, 4, & 5 in the action planning process should be done twice throughout the year between profile reports. If improvements are evident from the subsequent annual survey report, congratulations! Your team is moving in the right direction. Commence a similar process with another characteristic next year. Again, use the relevant tools for that characteristic in PART II.

Besides shifting focus to another characteristic to develop, the only other change that may be necessary is adding or removing survey participants. It is preferable to invite the same participants to complete successive surveys for consistency. But in practice, it's likely as time passes that there will be changes in the team and different stakeholders. Adjust for this by removing redundant participants and inviting new ones to offer their perspective.

By using the team profile and action plan, you'll be paying more attention to the people dimension of teamwork. The people dimension is the key to the All Black team's success and dominance in the world of rugby. Paying the same attention to the people dimension of teamwork will balance tasks and relationships. This is the way to build a great team. Without deliberate concentration—using the team profile and action plan—it's likely that the people dimension will be underdeveloped. This throttles team performance. The relationships in teams are what make the difference.

I wish you well on your team development journey.

The top 10 key points

1. There are five steps in the action-planning process.

2. The first step is to administer the team profile survey.

3. The team profile survey uses a 360-degree methodology.

4. Step two is to generate the team profile report.

5. The team profile report consists of 80 statements, categorized into the eight characteristics of the Team Identity model.

6. The third step is to create an agenda.

7. The agenda should focus on one under-performing characteristic.

8. Step four is to facilitate a team discussion.

9. The team discussion concentrates on the area with the most potential for improvement.

10. The final step is to develop some practical and realistic actions.

THANK YOU!

Thank you for joining me on the journey towards developing a high performing team. I hope you have found *WINNING TEAMS: The Eight Characteristics of High Performing Teams* useful!

If you loved the book and have a moment to spare, **I would really appreciate a short review on the site where you purchased.**

Your help in spreading the word is gratefully received!

NEED MORE HELP?

Team profile

If you wish to apply the team diagnostic I mentioned in PART III, please contact me direct at tim@winnersatwork.com.au and we can arrange this for you. It's a great place to start in your continuing journey to develop a high performing team.

Industry updates

If you would like to receive my monthly newsletter with interesting article and tools for leaders, please go to https://www.winnersatwork.com.au/latest-industry-updates/

Speaking & consulting

I speak regularly on this topic and others around the world. If you would like to engage me in your upcoming conference, contact me at tim@winnersatwork.com.au I am also available for consulting work too.

Useful leadership tools

Go to www.winnersatwork.com.au for some useful tools to assist you, your team, and organization.

OTHER BOOKS BY TIM BAKER

The 8 Values of Highly Productive Companies: Creating Wealth from a New Employment Relationship

The End of the Performance Review: A New Approach to Appraising Employee Performance

Attracting and Retaining Talent: Becoming an Employer of Choice

The New Influencing Toolbox: Capabilities for Communicating with Influence

Conversations at Work: Promoting a Culture of Conversation in a Changing Workplace

The End of the Job Description: Changing from a Job-focus to Performance-focus

Performance Management for Agile Organizations: Overthrowing the Eight Management Myths that Hold Businesses Back

Bringing the Human Being Back to Work: The 10 Performance and Development Conversations Leaders Must Have

If you would like to pre-order a copy of my upcoming book:

Making Empowerment Work: A New Approach to Maximizing Performance

Contact me at tim@winninersatwork.com.au

ABOUT TIM BAKER

Tim Baker is a thought leader, international consultant, and successful author. Tim is managing director of WINNERS-at-WORK Pty Ltd, which specializes in leadership development and performance improvement (www.winnersatwork.com.au).

He was recently voted one of *The Most Talented Global Training & Development Leaders* by the World HRD Congress, which is awarded by a distinguished international panel of professionals "who are doing extraordinary work" in the field of HRD. In 2018, Tim was a Finalist in the *Learning Professional of the Year* for the Asia Pacific Institute of Learning Professionals Awards. His consulting firm WINNERS-at-WORK Pty Ltd was listed in the *Top 10 Change Management Consulting Service Companies* in APAC 2020 (HR Tech Outlook).

Tim completed his Doctoral degree in 2005 at QUT. He has served on QUT Council for over 11-years.

Tim has conducted over 2,430 seminars, workshops, and keynote addresses to over 45,000 people in 12 countries across 21 industry groups and regularly writes for HR industry press. Tim can be contacted at tim@winnersatwork.com.au.

Tim lives in Brisbane, Australia with his wife Carol. He has two daughters.

CONNECT WITH TIM ONLINE

LinkedIn: https://www.linkedin.com/in/winnersatwork/

Facebook: https://www.facebook.com/winnersatworkptyltd

Twitter: https://twitter.com/winnersatwork

Instagram: https://www.instagram.com/winnersatwork/

Pinterest: https://www.pinterest.com.au/winnersatwork/

YouTube: https://www.youtube.com/channel/UCVkrLzgIP0rV5TUQitTT6sQ

SlideShare: https://www.slideshare.net/DrTimBaker

ACKNOWLEDGEMENTS

Thanks to David Kelly for editing the final chapter and providing the team profile tool. Thanks to Chris Burton for offering his expertise and editing CHAPTER 20. My thanks too to rugby greats Nick Farr-Jones, Tom Lawton, and Grant Fox for writing testimonials for the book and Commissioner Katarina Carroll of Queensland Police Service for the same. I also want to acknowledge Audrean Verr F. Lamoste for designing the cover for this book and Susan Veach for the internal design.

REFERENCES

1   Kerr, J. (2013). Legacy: What the All Blacks can teach us about the business of life. Constable: London.

2   Bull. A. (2015). The making of an All Black: How New Zealand sustains its rugby dynasty. *The Guardian*. Sourced at: https://www. theguardian.com/sport/blog/2015/sep/11/all-blacks-how-new-zealand-sustains-its-rugby-dynasty

3   Bull. A. (2015). The making of an All Black: How New Zealand sustains its rugby dynasty. *The Guardian*. Sourced at: https://www. theguardian.com/sport/blog/2015/sep/11/all-blacks-how-new-zealand-sustains-its-rugby-dynasty

4   Kerr, J. (2013). Legacy: What the All Blacks can teach us about the business of life. Constable: London.

5   Kerr, J. (2013). Legacy: What the All Blacks can teach us about the business of life. Constable: London.

6   Kerr, J. (2013). Legacy: What the All Blacks can teach us about the business of life. Constable: London.

7   Kerr, J. (2013). Legacy: What the All Blacks can teach us about the business of life. Constable: London.

8   Tuckman, B.W. & Jensen, A.C. (1977). Stages of small-group development revisited. Sage (December), https://doi.org/10.1177/105960117700200404

9   Baker, T. (2009). The 8 values of highly productive companies: Creating wealth from a new employment relationship. Brisbane: Australian Academic Press.

10 Kerr, J. (2013). Legacy: What the All Blacks can teach us about the business of life. Constable: London.

11 Cross, R.L., Yang, A., & Louis, M.R (2000). Boundary activities in boundary less organizations: A case study of a transformation to a team-based structure. *Human Relations*, 53(6), 841-857.

12 Cross, R.L., Yang, A., & Louis, M.R (2000). Boundary activities in boundary less organizations: A case study of a transformation to a team-based structure. *Human Relations*, 53(6), 841-857.

13 Smythe, J. (2017). Why are the All Blacks so good? Retrieved from https://www.ft.com/content/b5afe588-560b-11e7-80b6-9bfa4c1f83d2

14 Bennis, W (1993). An invented life: Reflections on leadership and change. Reading, MA: Basic Books.

15 Kerr, J. (2013). Legacy: What the All Blacks can teach us about the business of life. Constable: London.

16 Kerr, J. (2013). Legacy: What the All Blacks can teach us about the business of life. Constable: London.

17 This quote has also been attributed to Edward Everett Hale (1822–1909), an American author, poet, historian, and Unitarian minister.

18 Coleman, J.S. (1990). Foundations of social theory. Cambridge, MA: Harvard University Press.

19 Hakanen, M., & Soudunsaari, A. (2012). Building trust in high-performing teams. *Technology Innovation Management Review*, 2, 6.

20 Baker, T. & Warren, A. (2015). Conversations at work: Promoting a culture of conversation in the changing workplace. London: Palgrave Macmillan.

21 Edelman (2014) "2014 Edelman Trust Barometer." http://www.edelman.com.

22 Covey, S.M.R. & Merrill, R.R. (2006) The speed of trust: The one thing that changes everything. New York: Free Press.

23 http://www.psychologytoday.com/blog/trust-the-new-workplacecurrency/

201309/ten-ways-cultivate-work-relationships-and-grow-trust.

24 https://www.mindtools.com/pages/article/building-trust-team.
htm

25 https://en.wikiquote.org/wiki/Frank_Crane

26 Hsiao-Wen Ho, M., Ghauri, P.N., & Larimo, J.A. (2018).
Institutional distance and knowledge acquisition in international
buyer-supplier relationships: The moderating role of trust. *Asia
Pacific Journal of Management*, 35, 2, 427-447

27 https://www.cbremelbourne.com.au/wp-content/
uploads/2017/11/All-blacks-Poster_01.pdf

28 Kerr, J. Lessons from the All Blacks: Create a Team of Leaders
Part 2. Retrieved from https://teamupevents.co.nz/2016/06/blacks-
can-teach-us-developing-successful-team-part-2/

29 Goldsmith, M. (2010). Sharing leadership to maximize talent.
Harvard Business Review. Retrieved from https://hbr.org/2010/05/
sharing-leadership-to-maximize

30 Pink, D.H. (2009). Drive: the surprising truth about what
motivates us. New York: Riverhead Books.

31 Hakanen, M., Hakkinen, M., & Soudunsaari, A. (2015). Trust in
building high-performance teams—conceptual approach. *Electronic
Journal of Business Ethics and Organization Studies*. 20, 2, 43-53.

32 Baker, T.B. (2014). Attracting and retaining talent: Becoming an
employer of choice. London: Palgrave Macmillan.

33 Nelson, F. (2014). Firms slow to change with the times.
Retrieved from http://www.lawyersweekly.com.au/news/15588-
firms-slow-to-change-with-the-times

34 Baker, T.B. (2017). Performance management for agile
organizations: Overthrowing the eight management myths that
hold businesses back. London: Palgrave Macmillan.

35 Baker, T.B. (2017). Performance management for agile organizations: Overthrowing the eight management myths that hold businesses back. London: Palgrave Macmillan.

36 Robson, T. (2013). All Blacks keep it simple with training methods. Retrieved from http://www.stuff.co.nz/sport/rugby/all-blacks/8787948/All-Blacks-keep-it-simple-with-training-methods

37 Baker, T.B. (2016). The end of the job description: Shifting from a job-focus to a performance-focus. London: Palgrave Macmillan.

38 http://blog.readytomanage.com/top-10-most-valued-job-skills/

39 Wheeler, K. (2009). Agility skill acquisition in Rugby Union. PhD thesis.

40 Baker, T.B. (2016). The end of the job description: Shifting from a job-focus to a performance-focus. London: Palgrave Macmillan.

41 Kerr, J. (2013). Legacy: What the All Blacks can teach us about the business of life. Constable: London.

42 Kenny, G. (2018). Your corporate purpose will ring hollow if the company's actions don't back it up. (August) *Harvard Business Review*.

43 http://www.leadershipgeeks.com/team-mission-statements/

44 http://toolbox.hyperisland.com/team-purpose-culture

45 Baker, T. (2015). The new influencing toolkit: Capabilities to communicate with influence. London: Palgrave Macmillan.

46 https://www.gitadaily.com/sutra-6-words-shape-worlds-watch-your-words/

47 Adapted from Hartley, S. (2009). Project management: Principles, processes and practices (2nd ed.) Frenchs Forest: Pearson.

48 https://www.apm.org.uk/body-of-knowledge/delivery/integrative-management/stakeholder-management/

49 Kandola, A. (2017). What is NLP and what is it used for? Retrieved from https://www.medicalnewstoday.com/articles/320368.php

50 McLachlan, S. (2014). Most commonly made mistakes in stakeholder engagement. Retrieved from https://www.thoughtexchange.com/most-commonly-made-mistakes-in-stakeholder-engagement/

51 http://www.saylor.org/site/wp-content/uploads/2013/02/BUS208-1.2.7-Influencing-Skills-FINAL.pdf

52 https://www.mindtools.com/pages/article/newLDR_56.htm

53 Kerr, J. (2013). Legacy: What the All Blacks can teach us about the business of life. Constable: London.

54 O'Reilly, C.A. & Tushman, M.L. (2004). The ambidextrous organization. *Harvard Business Review*, April edition.

55 VUCA is an acronym – first used in 1987, drawing on the leadership theories of Warren Bennis and Burt Nanus to describe or to reflect on the volatility, uncertainty, complexity and ambiguity of general conditions and situations.

56 United States Chamber of Commerce (2008). Southwest's secret to a positive corporate culture: its employees. Retrieved June 24, 2008, from http://www.uschammber.com/bclc/sothwest.htm

57 Baker, T.B. (2013.). The end of the performance review: A new approach to appraising employee performance. London: Palgrave Macmillan.

58 Senge, P. (1999). The dance of change (A fifth discipline resource). New York: Random House.

59 https://www.frames.gov/partner-sites/emissions-and-smoke/educational-resources/case-studies/the-atlanta-incident/the-after-action-review/

60 Kerr, J. (2013). Legacy: What the all Blacks can teach us about the business of life. Constable: London.

61 Hunt, V., Layton, D. & Prince, S. (2015). Why diversity matters. Retrieved from https://www.mckinsey.com/business-functions/organization/our-insights/why-diversity-matters

62 Hunt, V., Layton, D. & Prince, S. (2015). Why diversity matters. Retrieved from https://www.mckinsey.com/business-functions/organization/our-insights/why-diversity-matters

63 Group Think is the practice of thinking or making decisions as a group, resulting typically in unchallenged, poor-quality decision-making.

64 Hunt, V., Layton, D. & Prince, S. (2015). Why diversity matters. Retrieved from https://www.mckinsey.com/business-functions/organization/our-insights/why-diversity-matters

65 Gompers, P. & Kovvali, S. (2018). The other diversity dividend. *Harvard Business Review*, June- July issue.

66 Gompers, P. & Kovvali, S. (2018). The other diversity dividend. *Harvard Business Review*, June- July issue.

67 Gompers, P. & Kovvali, S. (2018). The other diversity dividend. *Harvard Business Review*, June- July issue.

68 Gompers, P. & Kovvali, S. (2018). The other diversity dividend. *Harvard Business Review*, June- July issue.

69 Lorenzo, R. & Reeves, M. (2018). How and where diversity drives financial performance. *Harvard Business Review*.

70 Lorenzo, R. & Reeves, M. (2018). How and where diversity drives financial performance. *Harvard Business Review*.

71 Margerison, C. and McCann, D. (1995). Team management: Practical new approaches. Didcot, UK: Management Books.

72 Contact me at tim@winnersatwork.com.au if wish to undertake the TMP, either as an individual or the team.

73 If you would like more information about Team Management Systems, or to complete the Team Management Profile, please go to http://www.tms.com.au/

74 Baker, T. (2014). Attracting and retaining talent: Becoming an employer of choice. London: Palgrave Macmillan.

75 Kerr, J. (2013). Legacy: What the All Blacks can teach us about the business of life. Constable: London.

76 Kuchinke, K.P. (1999). Adult education towards what end? A philosophical analysis of the concept as reflected in the research theory and practice of human resource development. *Adult Education Quarterly*, 49 (4), 148–160. Maitland, I. (1994). The morality of the corporation. *Business Ethics Quarterly*, 4, 445–458.

77 Baker, T. (2014). Attracting and retaining talent: Becoming an employer of choice. London: Palgrave Macmillan.

78 https://www.theguardian.com/sport/2016/nov/03/all-blacks-skill-strength-the-breakdown

79 Contact Dr Tim Baker at tim@winnersatworkcom.au

80 Contact Dr Tim Baker at tim@winnersatworkcom.au